GUIDED MEDITATION

LIGHT OF VEDANTA PRESS

WITH

SWAMINI SVATMAVIDYANANDA

तद्विद्धि प्रणिपातेन परिप्रश्नेन सेवया

ISBN: 978-1-66641-448-6

Arsha Vijnana Gurukulam
1190 W 27th Ave, Eugene, OR 97405
For more information visit: https://www.arshavg.org

PUJYA SRI SWAMI DAYANANDAJI

Seeds of oneness sprout
'midst the mahāvākya clouds
upadeśa rains
liquefy all names and forms
reveal the Guru within.

DEDICATION

Dedicated with devotion to
Sri Swami Sakshatkrtananda ji
who has *rāga* only for *tyāga*

FOREWORD

arsha vijnana gurukulam

8570 Village Place
Suwanee, GA 30024
(470) 564-0644
arshavg.org

1190 W 27th Ave
Eugene, OR 97405
(541) 684-0322
arshavm.org

A book on meditation is much like a cookbook. Both discuss intricate techniques and have nice illustrations, and in both cases the desired results cannot be gained by just reading them. Just as one cannot satiate one's hunger by studying a recipe book, so too, one cannot read about meditation and hope to gain a tranquil mind.

What can one do to gain mastery over the mind? Two practices are discussed, *abhyāsa* and *vairāgya*. *Abhyāsa* is consistent practice through which one gains an inner distance between the mind and the "I" by repeatedly seeing nature of the self as whole and limitless. *Abhyāsa* can also include the practice whereby *mantra-japa* is perfected. *Vairāgya* is the cultivation of a disposition that helps one to see objects, events, and people dispassionately, without a charge. Over time *abhyāsa* and *vairāgya* help to tame the mind and shed distractions and addictions. The meditations and contemplations given in this book have been chosen to help a seeker to make steady progress in handling the mind with gentleness and self-compassion. Only when the mind is prepared in this manner can self-knowledge take root and abide in the heart.

I commend Neeru and Harinder for their hard work to bring this work to fruition. I also appreciate the student body, whose members are individually mentioned in the preface, for cheerfully pitching in with their time and expertise at short notice.

I hope that this book, along with the meditation practice, is useful to seekers everywhere.

Swamini Svatmavidyananda
Swami Dayananda Ashram
Rishikesh, India

KEY TO TRANSLITERATION

KEY TO TRANSLITERATION AND PRONUNCIATION OF SANSKRIT LETTERS

Sanskrit is a highly phonetic language and hence accuracy in articulation of the letters is important. For those unfamiliar with the *Devanāgari* script, the international transliteration is a guide to the proper pronunciation of Sanskrit letters.

अ	*a*	*(but)*	ट	*ṭa*	*(true)**3
आ	*ā*	*(father)*	ठ	*ṭha*	*(anthill)**3
इ	*i*	*(it)*	ड	*ḍa*	*(drum)**3
ई	*ī*	*(beat)*	ढ	*ḍha*	*(godhead)**3
उ	*u*	*(full)*	ण	*ṇa*	*(under)**3
ऊ	*ū*	*(pool)*	त	*ta*	*(path)**4
ऋ	*ṛ*	*(rhythm)*	थ	*tha*	*(thunder)**4
ॠ	*ṝ*	*(marine)*	द	*da*	*(that)**4
ऌ	*ḷ*	*(revelry)*	ध	*dha*	*(breathe)**4
ए	*e*	*(play)*	न	*na*	*(nut)**4
ऐ	*ai*	*(aisle)*	प	*pa*	*(put)* 5
ओ	*o*	*(go)*	फ	*pha*	*(loophole)**5
औ	*au*	*(loud)*	ब	*ba*	*(bin)* 5
क	*ka*	*(seek)* 1	भ	*bha*	*(abhor)**5
ख	*kha*	*(blockhead)**1	म	*ma*	*(much)* 5
ग	*ga*	*(get)* 1	य	*ya*	*(loyal)*
घ	*gha*	*(log hut)**1	र	*ra*	*(red)*
ङ	*ṅa*	*(sing)* 1	ल	*la*	*(luck)*
च	*ca*	*(chunk)* 2	व	*va*	*(vase)*
छ	*cha*	*(catch him)**2	श	*śa*	*(sure)*
ज	*ja*	*(jump)* 2	ष	*ṣa*	*(shun)*
झ	*jha*	*(hedgehog)**2	स	*sa*	*(so)*
ञ	*ña*	*(bunch)* 2	ह	*ha*	*(hum)*

ं	*ṁ*	*anusvara*	(nasalisation of preceding vowel)
ः	*ḥ*	*visarga*	(aspiration of preceding vowel)
*			No exact English equivalents for these letters
ऽ	'	*avagraha*	(indicates a dropped vowel - not pronounced)

1.	Guttural	–	Pronounced from throat
2.	Palatal	–	Pronounced from palate
3.	Lingual	–	Pronounced from cerebrum
4.	Dental	–	Pronounced from teeth
5.	Labial	–	Pronounced from lips

The 5th letter of each of the above class – called nasals – are also pronounced nasally.

PREFACE

sadāśivasamārambhāṃ śaṅkarācāryamadhyamām
asmadācāryaparyantāṃ vande guruparamparām
I venerate the entire lineage of gurus that started with Lord Shiva,
with Adi Shankara in the middle, right up to my own acharya.

Contemplation, *nidhidhyāsana,* which removes habitual orientations such as identification with the body-mind-sense complex, is a very important component of spiritual *sādhanā*. *Śravaṇa,* the committed pursuit of Vedanta through listening to a teacher repeatedly, gives us the understanding of our true nature. *Manana*, querying what has been heard, frees the knowledge from doubts, and *nididhyāsana*, repeated revelry in the vision of Vedanta as free, whole, and limitless, is needed when we understand the vision of Vedanta but have difficulty assimilating it as the truth of ourself.

As Pujya Swami Dayanandaji points out in the introduction to Chapter 6 in the Bhagavad-Gita Home Study, *dhyāna (*meditation) and *nididhyāsana (*contemplation) are essential spiritual practices (*sādhana*) for training the mind and internalizing the teachings of Vedanta. While listening to the guru unfolding the *śāstra*, an undisciplined mind may become distracted and unable to grasp the subtlety of the teachings. The practice of *dhyāna* disciplines the mind by making it capable of focused, sustained attention. Consequently, all distractions are set aside so that only thoughts of the teaching flow, thus preparing and steadying the mind to receive knowledge. *Nididhyāsana*, on the other hand, is the deep, repeated contemplation and assimilation of what has been heard, reflecting on and identifying with the truth of one's own nature as the limitless, sentient existence that upholds the entire universe. While the practice of *dhyāna* disciplines and steadies the mind, *nididhyāsana* helps assimilate the knowledge of the self gained through *śravaṇa* as the truth of oneself in a complete and error-free manner.

Sri Swaminiji, with her decades of experience interacting with many seekers all over the world, recently led a series of guided meditation sessions where she seamlessly incorporates both practices of *dhyāna* and *nididhyāsana*. In these meditations, Swaminiji holds the hand of the seekers and guides them step by step to the next level in preparing the mind to assimilate the teachings with greater ease.

A special feature of this book is that direct access to these sessions is available on Swaminiji's YouTube channel through hyperlinks and QR codes given at the end of each meditation. We feel privileged to express our gratitude to Sudhanshu Kute for the beautiful cover art and *Brahmacāriṇī* Shambhavee and Niyati Shah for the interior artwork. Jahnavi Iyer did wonders with her grammar skills and proofreading. The jack of all trades, Shambhavi, helped in many ways. Chris Almond was invaluable in helping navigate through the word-processing program.

It is very difficult to express in words the gratitude we feel for the selflessness and dedication that our teachers model for us. May this offering in the form of a book be a small token of our reverence at Swaminiji's lotus feet.

With all our gratitude and prostrations.

Neeru Aggarwal, Gurugram, India
Harinder Kaur Khalsa, Eugene, OR, USA
August 15th, 2025

MINDING THE MIND

A Poem by Swamini Svatmavidyananda

Let the mind wander,
Let it meander.
One who tries to catch it, will surely get caught
This is what the *Gurus* of yore have us taught.
Tis good to accept the things that cannot change
Past, present, and the future lie in this range.
Thoughts are like monkeys, they leap and fly at will
Or like the frogs who know not how to be still,
Dragonflies that flit with iridescent wings
Grasshoppers, crickets, and other jumping things.
Let the mind wander,
Let it meander.

Who's the one who sees, who is the one who knows
That the mind can't be still, on and on it goes?
Catch the catcher, the one who is really you
Then you discover there's nothing more to do.
Let the mind wander,
Let it meander.

The mind is not a threat; it cannot subdue you
You are free of it as you see it through and through.
With *Oṃ* as the *mantra*, the anchor and guide

Steer the boat home after an interesting ride
Let the mind wander,

Let it meander.

With consistent practice, the mind is dethroned
Dwelling in one's glory is a skill that's honed
When the mind wants to be included once more
Let it enter through the rear service door
Let the mind wander
Let it meander.

Now the mind, tamed and trained, is the shining one
A mirror reflecting the orb of the sun
Where knowledge of the self as joy without bounds
Frees one of all wants –it's as good as it sounds
Let the mind be a wonder,
Let it surrender.

TABLE OF CONTENTS

INTRODUCTION....1

SECTION I MEDITATION (*DHYĀNA*)

Foundation 16

Acceptance through Surrender 22

Oceanic Awareness....26

Cultivating Compassion 29

An Appointment With Myself 32

Acceptance Of The *Karmic* Order 34

I Am *Saccidānanda* 38

Human Nature Is An Extension Of Nature 41

Letting Go Of Limitations 44

Being Myself Is Effortless 48

The Limited And The Limitless 51

The Human Body Is *Isvarā's* Marvel 54

Relaxing In The Order 57

Take Away 64

Let There Be More Of You, Less Of Me 66

Darśan Is Abidance In The Self 70
Mānasa Pūjā: Mental Worship 72
I Am Comfortable Being Myself 76
Abiding In *Iśvara* 79
Acceptance, And Self-Compassion 82
SECTION II CONTEMPLATION (*NIDIDHYĀSANA*)
Discovering The *Sākṣin* (Witness) 89
I Am *Asaṅga*, The Changeless Awareness 93
Being Still 96
Relating To The Order 100
Jyotiṣām Jyotiḥ: The Light Of All Lights 104
The Truth Of Oneself 107
The Traveler And The Destination Are One 110
The Giver And The Given 113
Ever Connected, Never Alienated 116
Consciousness Is Not An Object 119
Meditating With The Wind 122
Nothing Is Outside Of *Īśvara* 124
Surrender To The Ocean Of Auspiciousness 128

What Is, *Is* 131
I Am Free Of The Role, But The Role Depends On Me 134
I Am The Witness Consciousness 138
I Am Home With Myself 142
SECTION III QUICK MEDITATIONS FOR BUSY PEOPLE
Being Oneself 148
Relieving Stress 150
Decision Making 154
Meditation On Anger 158
Reconnecting With Oneself 161
Relaxation 164
Removing Obstacles 167
APPENDIX 171
GLOSSARY 175

When I go with the flow, I am in harmony with everything. When I practice being in the flow, I become the flow; I am one with Īśvara.

INTRODUCTION

The vision of Vedanta is to understand oneself as non-separate from *Īśvara*[1], the cause of the universe. While this truth is gained by *śravana*–listening to the teachings of the Upanishads from a qualified teacher–meditation plays a vital role in preparing the mind for gaining self-knowledge.

There are two conditions of the mind that inhibit the assimilation of the knowledge of oneself as whole, limitless and free. The first one is *vikṣepa*, distraction. The mind, which is always in motion, has to be disciplined to have *sthairya*, steadfastness. It must be trained to be able to focus and assimilate the teachings of the *śāstra*. The second one is *laya*, resolution, or sleep. When the mind resolves, instead of self-knowledge, sleep arrives. Therefore, the mind should be relaxed, yet awake.

In the 6th chapter of the Bhagavad-Bhagavad-Gita, Arjuna, advised by Lord Krishna to discipline the mind through meditation, says that since the mind is constantly moving, catching hold of the mind and asking it to stay with one thought is as difficult as catching a fistful of air. Lord Krishna advises him to train the mind through *abhyāsa*, repetition of the mantra, and *vairagya*, letting go of *rāga-dveṣa* (strong preferences and prejudices). During the course of the day, the mind leaps from thought to thought, seemingly without any connection. Although we generally say that thoughts come in quick succession without rhyme or reason, usually there is both. Often the connection between two apparently disjointed thoughts is buried in the unconscious mind. The *vāsanā* of the past gets triggered by sights, sounds, smells, words, ideas, and interactions with people in the present.

---

[1] *Īśvara, Bhagavan, Brahman*–often translated as God–is understood as the conscious, sentient, limitless being, the all-encompassing intelligence and presence from which everything arises, by which everything is pervaded, and into which everything ultimately resolves.

Often one is unaware of the trigger, but only sees the aftermath in the form of thoughts eclipsing the mind, and preventing it from being in the present.

Furthermore, the sense-organs, powered by strong *rāga-dveṣa,* hijack the *antaḥkaraṇa* into following them down the rabbit-hole of the sense-objects that drive one senseless. What one wants is the infinite, which is not an object, and which is already attained, as it is the nature of oneself. Due to self-ignorance, one chases the infinite everywhere except where it resides: in the heart of the seeker. Therefore, one does not have a say over the ways of the mind, which is in the hands of disjointed thoughts. This flow of discordant thoughts is called *vijātīyavṛttipravāha.* A salient objective of *dhyāna*, meditation, is to train the mind to have a say over the thoughts by telling it what to think. The mind is put on the diet of a mantra that one repeats mentally over and over again, bringing the mind back each time it moves away. Therefore, the mantra converts disconnected thoughts into *sajātīyavṛttipravāha,* a flow of same or similar thoughts. In this way, the mind gets disciplined and is available for the pursuit of the knowledge of the limitless Brahman as oneself.

The practice of meditation disciplines, focuses, and quietens the mind, converting it into a fitting instrument of self-inquiry and making it more receptive to the teachings of Vedanta. Self-knowledge takes place in the mind, but not by the mind as an agent. Since the mind is a receptacle rather than the agent of self-knowledge, it must be honed to be a clear, tranquil and focused instrument of knowledge.

The Definition of Meditation

Various spiritual traditions have different practices of meditation. In the Hindu tradition, meditation is entirely God-centric. This is already evident in the very definition of meditation–*saguṇabrahma viṣaye mānasavyāpāraḥ*–mental activity, for which the subject-matter is God, *Īśvara*. In the Vedic tradition, meditation is defined not just as a theory, or a series of techniques of watching the breath or the mind, but as a specific type of mental activity centered on *Bhagavān*, *Īśvara*. *Mānasavyāpāra* is mental activity. Mental activity could range from daydreaming about winning the lottery to critiquing others, stewing in one's emotions, or feeling victimized by others. However, in this context, the *viṣaya*, subject matter, of the mental activity is *saguṇa-Brahma*.

Brahma means *Bhagavān: Brahman* which is as-though endowed with attributes of the power of creation, *māyāśakti*. Brahman possesses the power to project, sustain, and resolve the universe, as well as the power to manifest in the form of the laws and as *niyantṛ*, the controller of everything–this is *saguṇa Brahma*. From the standpoint of the individual, this *Bhagavān*, this *Īśvara*, seems distant and not locally available. The Upaniṣads, therefore, refer to Brahman as tat, "that," not "this". Names and forms are seen; the things we refer to as "this" are locally available for objectification, but Brahman is not. Yet, without *Bhagavān*, no name or form can exist; nothing can exist or function, starting with one's own body-mind-sense complex. Therefore, meditation is connecting to *Īśvara* mentally.

Why Meditate upon *Īśvara*?

When we speak of meditation in the context of Vedanta, a common question arises: why seek a connection at all? After all, we are all *Īśvara*. All that is here–known and unknown –is pervaded by *Īśvara*, *īśāvāsyaṃ idaṃ sarvaṃ*. If this is the case, then why seek connection with *Īśvara*? Why pray, visit temples, or engage in mental connection? Who is the one praying, and to whom? Am I praying to myself? The answer lies in addressing the sense of alienation from the whole that is universally felt. Although there is no real disconnection, one often feels separated from *Bhagavān*. The need for connection arises not from an actual lack of connection but from the subjective experience of separation on the part of the *jīva*, the individual. This feeling of separation from the source of the universe causes sorrow, fear, and pain, which are the ingredients of *saṃsāra*. It begins with the feeling that *Īśvara* is everything, while one is a nobody; *Īśvara* is distant and powerful, while the *jīva* is powerless and far away.

If this disconnection were real, no mental activity focused on *Bhagavān* would help. This disconnection is deeply felt. It is a notion that is not objectively real, yet impossible to dismiss.

This universal experience of alienation–from the *jagat*, the world, from other people, other *jīvas*, and ultimately from *Īśvara*, the source of the universe–cannot be denied. At the same time, it cannot be affirmed as absolute either. That order of reality which cannot be categorically or objectively affirmed, nor experientially denied, is known as *mithyā*. *Mithyā* is the empirical reality dependent on Brahman. Just as the pot depends upon clay for its existence, and the ornament depends upon gold, so too the jagat depends upon *sat, Brahman*. Taking *mithyā* to be real causes alienation and sorrow: separation anxiety. This insecurity begins in early childhood with questions like "Where is mummy? Where is daddy?", and continues even into old age, as one seeks connection after connection. Since whatever one contacts is *anitya*, finite, the insecurity does not go away. The separation-anxiety that one recognized in childhood as alienation from the primary caregivers cannot be resolved until one ultimately discovers and connects with the parents of the universe; In the opening prayer to the Raghuvaṃśa, poet Kalidasa writes: *jagataḥ pitarau vande pārvatīparameśvarau,* which means, "I bow to the parents of the universe in the form of Goddess Parvati and Lord Parameshvara."

Therefore, no matter what one accomplishes in life, without developing a strong connection to *Īśvara*, one cannot neutralize the insecurity and sense of alienation centered on the self, which are the source of loneliness, sorrow, and fear. Alienation is *mithyā,* which means that which is not totally real. If it were real, it would persist in all three states of being; whether one is sleeping, dreaming, or waking, the sense of alienation would be there because that is which is *sat*, real, is unchanging and cannot be negated. However, in sleep no one feels alienated. One is in the lap of *Īśvara;* there is experience of oneness. No one wants to wake up from a peaceful deep sleep, because one enjoys the state of non-alienation.

Yet in this enjoyment, the mind has retreated to a causal state and cannot articulate the experience. The enjoyment of sleep is best recollected afterwards. In sleep, there is total oneness, and even the *pramātṛ*, the *ahaṅkāra* as the knower, is not around.

The sense of alienation is felt painfully only during the waking state. Meditation offers a U-turn–a turning back to oneself, away from focusing on the *anātman*, the "not-I." Where is this self? Not locally available. The body is "I", yes, but I am more than the body. The mind is "I", but the "I" envelops and transcends the mind and senses. The one looking for the "I" is the "I". That which cannot be seen is the "I"; the seer is the "I". The truth of the seer is the "I", even when nothing is witnessed or seen.

This "I" must be understood as non-separate from the maker, the creator of the *jagat*. Meditation interrupts duality, allowing deep connection with this truth. It is a homecoming, or, rather, an "Oṃ-coming." One is at home when one is one with the truth of Om. In sleep, this happens effortlessly; during the day, meditation helps stave off sorrow and strife by reconnecting with that unity.

Purifying the *Antaḥkaraṇa*

To support this reconnection, there needs to be a process of inner purification: the practice of *nāmajapa,* repeating the name of one's *īṣṭadevatā* (*Īśvara* in the form of one's chosen deity–such as *Hari, Śiva*, or Goddess *Durgā). Nāmajapa* acts as an internal soap that cleanses *antaḥkaraṇa*, the inner instrument, of the daily grime of *rāga-dveṣa*. When these preferences and prejudices go unfulfilled, when one cannot avoid what is unwanted or obtain what is desired, anger, delusion, greed, and other challenging emotional states arise and proliferate. Before long, the person becomes a ball of stress.

Śauca, cleanliness, is an important value highlighted in the Upanishads, *Yogasutras*, and the *Bhagavad-Bhagavad-Gita*. *Śauca* is twofold: for the body, there is soap–many kinds of soap–and for the mind, there is meditation, various kinds of meditation for cleaning mental cobwebs. This cleaning is done daily.

Just as one brushes the teeth or takes a shower daily, so too meditation has to be a regular practice. Another important reason to meditate is to keep the mind fit. When one goes to the gym or does yoga, the muscles are supple, and the body can take in some stress without losing immunity or falling apart. Similarly, when the mind is strengthened against the constant attacks of *rāga* and *dveṣa*, in the inner Kurukshetra– battleground– of the heart, the practice of meditation keeps the mind steady and tranquil.

Bringing Oneself to the Present

Meditation allows one to abide in the present. The ability to stay in the present is a gift one an give oneself. The present is a place where sorrow and strife cannot exist. Anxiety comes from thinking about the past or the future. The present is gone because one is busy regretting the past or dreading the future. The present is right now. "Now" is very interesting. How long is "now?" Are you here now? Yes. What about now? Yes. Now? Yes. Now? Yes. The "now" is unending. Now is not a length of time; now is, in fact, the ruler that measures time itself. It is timeless. If asked, "Are you sad now?" the answer will never be yes. Even if someone says, "Yes, I'm sad now," it must be pointed out that that was then; that moment has already gone. Now is free of sorrow, now is *Īśvara*, now is you, and meditation makes one abide in the now. Right now, there is freedom. Right now, there is wholeness. Right now, there is connection. Right now, there is no anxiety. Right now, "I" is all there is, all there is now. When one is one with now, one is one with *Īśvara*, because "now" is another name for *Īśvara*. "I am now" is a modern *mahāvākya*, so to speak.

Rediscovering One's Identity

Another reason to meditate is to discover one's identity, or rather, to rediscover one's identity. If asked, "Who are you?" generally, in society, one will say, "I am so and so," giving a name. The next identity is the answer to the question, "What do you do?"–one identifies as an engineer, a writer, a teacher, a health worker, and so on.

Then come relational identities, such as daughter, son, spouse, mother, and father. Even in official documents, identities are defined in relation to others. There are also identities regarding one's possessions, such as homeowner or club member. But these are tenuous identities; if one defines oneself by height, science shows that is not constant. As one grows older, the height becomes less, sometimes one is hunched over. Who am I? Height is not constant. Weight is not constant. Hair is not constant, provided one still has it in middle age. Relationships are not constant. All identities are time-bound, but the heart is geared towards discovering the infinite as oneself.

Therefore, the primary purpose of meditation is to discover and be at home with an identity that will never go away: to discover oneself as a *bhakta,* a devotee. From the standpoint of the body-mind-sense complex, one is a devotee, but seen through the vision of self-knowledge, one is non-separate from *Īśvara*. The identity of a *bhakta* is as-though there even after *ātmajñāna.* After gaining self-knowledge. One is a *jñānī-bhakta*, a *bhakta* who knows that everything is one, that one is non-separate from *Īśvara*. The identity of the *bhakta* is intimately discovered in meditation. When this happens, life becomes much easier, because one becomes a devotee-son, a devotee-daughter, a devotee-spouse, a devotee-co-worker, employee, employer, mother, or father. This is very important because it teaches us that the devotee "I", who is connected to *Īśvara,* is performing the roles of mother, father, son, daughter, sister, brother, spouse, co-worker, employer, employee, and so on. Interpersonal problems belong to the roles, not to the person. As long as one is firmly identified with the devotee, they do not overpower the person. The person and the role are one and the same, the role is non-separate from the person, however, the person is not the role. The person is the devotee, devoted to *Bhagavān*. The problems of the role do not roll on to the person. Meditation is therefore a useful auxiliary aid in self-discovery and self-growth.

How to Meditate

In the 5th and the 6th chapters of the Bhagavad-Gita, Lord Krishna gives Arjuna basic instructions for meditation. Lord Krishna says that the practice of meditation allows one to have a say over the ways of the mind. The mind is a blessing. It helps to think, to navigate various situations, to infer, to conclude, and to make the right choices in life. Mind management is the art of minding the mind in the face of challenging and strong emotions. The mind is a privilege and should not be turned into a slave of the recalcitrant *rāga-dveṣa*. This is the teaching in the Bhagavad-Gita.

Posture

samaṃ kāyaśirogrīvaṃ dhārayannacalaṃ sthiraḥ
saṃprekṣya nāsikāgraṃ svaṃ diśaścānavalokayan (BG 6.13)
Holding the body, head, and neck in a single and straight line, steady, firm and unmoving, may one fix the gaze upon the tip of the nose, without gazing in all directions.

Meditation starts with the body taking on the correct posture with the head, neck, and back in a single straight line. This posture is held unchangingly for the duration of the meditation. Having fixed the gaze on the tip of one's own nose, not looking in any direction, the eyes are softly closed, and the gaze is as though directed towards the tip of one's own nose, meaning the eyeballs are not restless behind the closed eyes.

Breathing

prāṇāpānau samau kṛtvā nāsābhyantaracāriṇau (BG 5.27)
Making the inhalation and exhalation more or less of equal length.

We begin with stabilizing the breath. Take some breaths, not even deep breaths, just a normal breathing pattern, but make the inhalations as long as the exhalations so that there is something to pay attention to, and the mind naturally becomes calm and quiet. This is very important. Then, there is an intriguing injunction before the *japa*.

Keep the External World, External

Sparśān kṛtvā bahir bāhyān । *(BG 5.27)*

Placing the external sense-objects outside.

Lord Krishna urges the meditator to keep the external world external. Why is it called the external world? Because it is outside. Then, how can one keep what is already external outside? The mind has residues, which meditation cleans up, and paradoxically the mind has to be relatively cheerful and cleaned up in order to be tranquil. Having kept the external world outside of oneself, outside of the meditation situation, is important because it is assumed that the meditating person brings with them a whole gamut of assumptions, notions, fears and sorrows from the past, and that is first kept outside in order to be able to be present with oneself in order to do the *japa*.

How to Gain Absorption in *Japa*

There are certain pointers given in the Upanishads and the Bhagavad-Bhagavad-Gita about doing *japa*. For example, we focus the mind on the chant, *Oṃ namaḥ śivāya*, but also focus on the space between the two chants, because that is where distraction tends to take place. *Oṃ namaḥ śivāya* is easy. Next, *Oṃ namaḥ śivāya*, also easy–*Oṃ namaḥ śivāya*. The mind is told to think *Oṃ namaḥ śivāya* constantly and keep other thoughts at bay. Every thought should be *Oṃ namaḥ śivāya*. It goes very well for the first four *Oṃ namaḥ śivāya*, then what is the fifth thought? "Is anything happening?" "Am I wasting my time?" From such distractions, the mind is repeatedly and gently brought back.

yato yato niścarati manaścañcalamasthiram ।

tatastato niyamyaitadātmanyeva vaśaṁ nayet ॥ *(BG 6.26)*

As the unsteady mind keeps moving away (from the chant)
bring it back repeatedly and gain mastery over it.

Just as a mother would gently bring back the toddler straying towards the traffic, so too one brings the wayward mind back to the chant.

Focusing on the spaces between the chants, where distraction tends to take place, is a good technique to steady the mind. No matter how many times the mind wanders, it is brought back. In fact, one cannot complain that the mind wanders because wandering is the nature of the mind.

asaṃśayaṃ mahabaho mano durnigrahaṃ calam ।
abhyāsena tu kaunteya, vairagyeṇa ca gṛhyate ॥ *BG 6.35*
Doubtlessly, O Mighty Armed One, the mind is difficult to manage and unsteady. It can, however, be mastered with repeated practice (of *japa*) and the cultivation of dispassion.

Lord Krishna agrees with Arjuna's complaint that the mind is difficult to subdue. Yes, this mind has to be moving. If it is not motion, it is not the mind. Otherwise, how will one perceive, how will one have quick reflexes, how will one jump out of a dangerous situation? It is because the mind keeps moving that perception and response to situations are possible. Here, the mind is not being stopped from moving, but it is told to move in a certain way. It is given a thought, and whenever it is distracted, the mind is gently brought back.

How to Use This Book

The guided meditations transcribed in this book teach how to meditate with step-by-step instructions, encapsulating the knowledge of the self in each meditation. Readers and listeners will learn:

- how to maintain a posture conducive to meditation.
- how to use the breath to bring the wandering mind back to the mantra.
- how to use various techniques to sharpen the focus of the mind.
- how to contemplate upon the truth of oneself as *sat-cit-ānanda.*

The self to be discovered is whole, limitless, and free. Although abiding in a finite body-mind-sense complex with all its limitations, tears, fears, likes dislikes, and disappointments, the self remains unaffected. Nothing can touch the *ātman*.

Each meditation will go deeper into clearing the obstacles in the heart and mind that may hinder the discovery of oneself as Brahman.

The best way to practice these meditations is to listen to them regularly– ideally, daily– and to contemplate upon the words by bringing them back to mind. Why, then, a book? Having the transcriptions available allows one to revisit specific passages, reflect more deeply, and to focus on particular aspects of spiritual growth that resonate. It is hoped that reading the words helps internalize the teachings, contemplate their meaning at one's own pace, and return to sections that speak most directly to one's journey. Furthermore, engaging with the material through both listening and reading supports multimodal learning–an approach that uses multiple senses and learning preferences to deepen understanding and retention. One can even write out the meditations to assimilate them more deeply, or read them aloud to make them more memorable, so that those healing words can be recalled quickly whenever needed.

tridalamtriguṇākāraṃ trinetraṃ ca triyāyuṣaṃ I
trijanma pāpasaṃhāram ekabilvaṃ śivārpaṇaṃ II

SECTION I
MEDITATION (*DHYĀNA*)

O Lord,
lift me from the
doldrums of discontent
and the onslaught
of unrepentant fortune
take me away
from the blame-game
of distrust inopportune.
Let me blossom,
a lotus untouched
by the *saṃsāra*-sludge
soaring like an
eagle on high
let me freely fly
the *cidākāśa* sky.

Meditator, meditation, and the object of meditation, are all non-separate from consciousness. Awareness morphs, as it were, into the meditator, dhyātṛ. Then I can say I am meditating now–dhyāyati iva, as though meditating. Now I am distracted, as though moving away, lelāyati iva.

When I let go, there is less of a
sense of burden, and I can heave
a sigh of relief. I am part of the
vast order; this body-mind-sense
complex is part of the order,
which is a manifestation of Īśvara.

The seat should be stable and comfortable such that one doesn't need to move or wriggle too much during the meditation. Establishing the seat itself takes a little time because one is not really used to sitting still. But once it is established over a period of practice, it is called *āsanasiddhi:* accomplishment of the posture. It is recommended that one starts sitting still like this at least for 48 minutes per day. 48 minutes is a Mandala. If you are able to achieve stillness in the body for 48 minutes, you have *āsanasiddhi.*

The place for meditation, likewise, also should not be too high because there will be a fear of falling and one will not be able to go too deep. Again, the seat must not be too low, as though one is inside a pit, because then again there is perhaps a fear of feeling claustrophobic. The traditional seat for the meditation is made on a well-swept floor with what is called *kusha* grass: a cushion of a little bit of *kusha* grass on top of which deer skin is placed, from a deer that died a natural death. The deer's skin is sacred because the deer symbolizes everything that is gentle, non-violent, non-interfering, and calm. This tells us the kind of temperament that one must have going into the meditation.

The deer skin is also seen as a purifier. So, sitting on the deer skin, which is free of insects thanks to the *kusha* grass, one feels safe, one feels pure and one is in a mood to meditate. The posture is important because it allows for a certain stability during the meditation. The head, neck, body, and the spine are in a single straight line and this is important to note because when there is absorption the head tends to droop downwards. Therefore, we make a point to hold this posture without moving. The eyes are softly closed, the hands are gently clasped on the lap with the thumbs touching. This again gives a certain stability to the posture. The gaze is soft. The eyeballs under the closed eyelids do not flutter or go from side to side. They're focused gently, forward and downward as though one would be looking at the tip of one's nose. One can see from this elaborate preparation that the whole point of meditation is to enable one to enter an internal process.

One stabilizes the breathing in the next step. Ideally, the breath is not forced. One is neither breathing too hard, nor breathing in a shallow manner. The length of the inhalation is roughly the same as the length of the exhalation. Stabilizing the breathing in this manner seems to have an effect again on the posture and on the general temperament. The mind quietens down. One feels more present, more connected to oneself. This is also a good device to use to be aware of the breathing, especially if one feels sleepy during the meditation.

The next step is a strange one: the advice is to keep the external world external. What can this possibly mean? The external world is so called because it's already outside. So what is this injunction that is received to keep what is outside, outside? How is this even possible to do? I visualize a range of mountains. In relation to these mountains I find that I am an objective, non-demanding person. In other words, I do not want the mountains to be a certain way. I do not expect them to be of a certain height. I'm just happy looking at them as they are. The mountains do not evoke a strong response in terms of my expectations. Next, I visualize a flowing river. Again, in relation to the river, the heart is open, perhaps even joyous. I find that I am an appreciative, non-demanding person in connection to the river.

What about people? Can I have this demeanor toward them? Can I retain this feeling of being an objective, non-demanding person with relation to people? Perhaps toward people in general, one can have the same objectivity if one does not carry prejudices based on race, gender, nationality, and other demographic factors. But what about people that are close to me?

I visualize the mother. This is exactly how she was or is in my perception. The words "in my perception" are important to use in this exercise because I give myself the benefit of

doubt; I could be right, but again, my perception need not be right. This is how the mother is, the mother was.
Retaining the care and love I have for the mother, I let go of expectations that she should be different, that she should have been different. This is done by my consciously granting her the freedom to be exactly how she is, how she was. This is how the mother was. This is how the mother is.

I do the same thing with the father. This is exactly how he was or is in my perception. I grant the father complete freedom consciously to be who he is or was. In so doing, I gain freedom with regard to the unrequited expectations in connection with the Father. One can do this for a spouse, significant other, child, friend, or anybody in one's life. By giving them the freedom to be to be who they are and letting go in the process, one finds that one is letting go of the hold of expectations with regard to the person.

We can see how there are two sets of parents in everyone's lives. One set is of course outside, but the other set is inside– internalized, rather– in the form of unrequited feelings, expectations, and frustrations. The step of taking the time to grant the person the freedom is important because it is a way of unloading the stowaways from one's head: people who are outside of oneself but who have crept inside and have gone under the skin, as it were, in the form of unrequited expectations. Keeping them where they belong outside gives a space, a vast inner space, which is important for meditation, important for discovering the meditator.

What about this body? Is this also external to me or is it internal to me? I observe the body part by part, starting with the head and the face. Allow the body parts that are called to soften and relax, just by being aware of them: the head, neck, and shoulders, I just observe.

I observe the right arm, the right elbow, the forearm, hand, and right fingers. I observe the left arm elbow, forearm, hand, and left fingers. I observe the front of the torso, the

chest, the stomach, and the abdomen. I observe the back of the torso: the upper back, mid back, lower back, and hips. I just observe. Now I observe the legs.
Starting with the right side, I observe the right hip, right thigh, knee the muscles below the knee, the calf muscles ankle and foot. I do the same observation on the left side: left hip, left thigh, left knee, calf, ankle, and foot.

This is how the body is. It is like the people in my life; there are many things about this body that I would like to be different but which I cannot change, such as the height, general weight, and predilection to certain ailments.

This is how the body is. If after this externalization process, I still have a wish for things or people to change, I offer it in the form of a prayer. Hey *Bhagavan*, O Lord, please give me the serenity and the grace to accept the things that I cannot change. Please give me the courage to change the things that I can. Above all, please give me the wisdom to know the difference between the things I can change and between those that I cannot. A wish that is not acted upon can causes frustration. Prayer is an action. So once one has prayed, there is no more frustration.

I now turn to watch the breathing, the *prāna*. Without altering the breath and making it fast or slow, I just observe the breath. In some traditions, watching the breath itself is meditation, but for us, it is a step to becoming familiar with the meditator, the one who wields the power to breathe.

Next, I observe the senses, and for today I observe the sense of touch as it is all pervasive throughout the body. I observe the hips on the seat on the chair, I observe the legs touching one another, the hands touching one another, the clothes touching the body, the upper and lower lips touching one another, and the tongue touching the teeth. To highlight the sense of touch, I half-open the eyes and gently let the upper eyelid descend upon the lower, observing that touch. There is nothing forced in this, and I do this once again: I half open the eyes and softly, gently close them. Whatever I can observe is external to me.

I now move to the watch mind, a powerful instrument, a reflection of all the thoughts, and a receptacle for the thoughts. I just watch the mind without chasing the thoughts or shunning the thoughts by just watch the mind.

A watched mind is a quiet mind. Observing the thoughts, I can see that they come and go. I can be myself and watch them without getting involved in them. I am the *sākṣin*, the witness of the body-mind-sense complex. I am uninvolved, *asaṅga*. If there are words to hear and the ears are functioning, they are heard; there is no will involved in hearing.

Hare Krishna, Hare Krishna, Krishna Krishna, Hare Hare.

In this prepared mind I place the chant. The chant is nothing other than a medium through which to connect with the total. The meditation is *saguṇa-brahma-viṣaya-mānasa-vyāpāra:* mental activity, a guided mental activity whose object is *Īśvara*. The observer is *Īśvara;* the truth of the individual is *Īśvara*, the whole, the collective, the total. The individual relates to the total, just like a tree relates to the forest. The tree is the forest, as it is already connected to the forest, but in the process of meditation, the connection between the jīva and *Īśvara* can be taken for granted. Therefore this connection is highlighted in the form of a chant. If you have your own mantra, you can use that. Otherwise, we can just use the mantra *Oṃ Īśāya namaḥ*. Unto *Īśā,* the overlord, the one who is all-in-all, I offer my surrender. The chant is placed in the mind, consciously. The breath and the voice are not silently involved. The chant is not synchronized with the breath. Chant silently and mentally now. Stop chanting and observe the spaces between the chants as I chant:
Oṃ Īśāya namaḥ Oṃ Īśāya namaḥ Oṃ Īśāya namaḥ Oṃ Īśāya namaḥ Oṃ Īśāya namaḥ Oṃ Īśāya namaḥ Oṃ Īśāya namaḥ Oṃ Īśāya namaḥ Oṃ Īśāya namaḥ Oṃ Īśāya namaḥ

Allow the chanting to come to a close. The chanting takes away the difference between the observer and the observed. If the chanting is successful, there is a sense of absorption.

Absorption is *laya*, the observer is *Īśvara*, that which is observed is *Īśvara*, and the chant itself *Īśvara*. Where is this *Īśvara*? The meditator is *Īśvara*. The truth is *Īśvara*. The conscious presence which pervades the body-mind-sense complex as the observer is nothing but *Īśvara:* the eye of the eye, the ear of the ear, the mind of the mind. I allow that presence to overpower reason, logic and all the categories in the mind.

I allow this presence to pervade that I, so that with every meditation I have a new rebirth –a renewed understanding of who I am, who this "I" is. I allow the 'I-ness' to be bathed in the presence, to melt in the presence most sacred, most holy, that which the Sufi called "the beloved" because it is the most near to oneself and the most sought after by all. If you are comfortable in rediscovering yourself, acknowledge it: "I am comfortable being myself, which means that I do not need any comforting from the outside." When you are ready, you can open your eyes. Oṃ *śāntiḥ śāntiḥ śāntiḥ*.

To access the live session, click **HERE** or scan the QR code given below:

ACCEPTANCE THROUGH SURRENDER

Meditation is an offering, a release of one's desires and wants. It is an acknowledgement and articulation of one's helplessness. As with every practice, there is preparation. The seat is firm, stable, and comfortable. The eyes are softly closed and the hands are clasped in front of the lap. The gaze is as though focused on the tip of one's nose through closed eyes, forward and steady. The breathing is soft, even, and gentle.

I allow the breath to bring my awareness to the body, inhabiting the body by being fully present. With every in-breath I am in the now, here, and arriving, with every out-breath I feel the body solid, heavy, centered, and grounded. I observe the body from head to the toe as though I am seated in front of a big mirror. I observe the body on my own at my own pace, starting with the head and ending at the toes.

Now, I gently shift the observation from the body to the sense of touch. To highlight the sense of touch, I half-open the eyes and notice the upper eyelid softly alighting on the lower eyelid. Once again, I half-open the eyes and softly close them, noticing the sense of touch. Elsewhere, clothes touch the body. The hands touch one another. The legs touch one another. The feet touch the floor. The tongue touches the teeth. The presence of the sense of touch is just that: nothing but presence, awareness, "I", *aham*. The "I" is all pervasive, free of sorrow, guilt and hurt.

Yet, as I move to observe the mind, I find that there is a big gap between the understanding of myself as whole and free and the individual, the *jīva*, characterized by helplessness. The cry for help and the acknowledgement of my own helplessness becomes a bridge to *Īśvara*. This cry is nothing but a mental prayer. The prayer, one must remember, is not just an expression of helplessness, but also an acceptance of what is, of everything which cannot be altered, at least for now.

Acceptance is a last resort when nothing works, when everything that I know and have tried has stopped giving me any form of relief and has stopped allowing me the hubris of feeling that I control my life. When everything in my life comes to a grinding stand still, despite my best intentions and efforts, I acknowledge my helplessness. Hey *Bhagavan*, what I see unfolding before me is an unending flow of your presence in the form of the law of karma. Help me to understand that. Help me to accept situations which do not go my way.

This helplessness that I am now coming to terms with has a long and checkered history. At birth, I was helpless. In the mother's womb, I was helpless. As a baby, I was totally helpless and dependent upon the caregivers, the mother, the father, or the relatives. I was subject to the idiosyncrasies of the caregivers, inconsistencies of the parents, and their own likes and dislikes. Being a victim of their desires, not understanding anything myself, I have seesawed from blaming the caregivers to blaming myself. Sometimes a victim, sometimes a martyr, I find that I cannot make peace with the past. Hey *Bhagavan*, I am apprehensive of the future.

The present stretches before me like an untrodden, uninhabited, landscape because I am too preoccupied with the past and the future, with my own omissions and commissions and others' omissions and commissions towards me. I am preoccupied with my own guilt and hurt.

I am nothing but a piece of flotsam in the ocean of creation, tossed about by the waves of hurt and guilt, utterly helpless, victimized by the past, and terrorized by the future. I acknowledge my helplessness. Oh father of the universe, oh mother, relieve me of the burden, of the composite hurt and guilt that I have been carrying needlessly lifetime after lifetime. All the things of the past births that I have done, may they dry up in your forgiving gaze.

kṣantavyo me'parādhaḥ śiva śiva śiva bho, śrī mahādeva śambho

I pray for my omissions and commissions in this life. I could have understood my mother better, I could have been more compassionate towards my father and my siblings. I could have been less reactive, more understanding, more open, and less defensive. I consciously gather these omissions like seashells on the shore and put them in your lap, O Mother, O Father of the universe.

May you transform these omissions into a work of art which tells the story of my life. May all the hurts, real and perceived, and all slings and arrows of outrageous fortune be washed in the waters of your compassion. May I be cleansed of all the inconsistencies and the lasting scars of my childhood.

In that compassionate gaze, may I understand that I was not at fault. May I learn to forgive myself. May I forgive others whose actions I have not yet been able to understand fully. I do not know what the future holds. I do not know the ways of karma, my own karma, and the karma of others with whom I am linked. I do not know what the morrow brings and whether I will be equipped to deal with it. I ask for the gift of your mercy to have the strength to be able to be in the present.

kṣantavyo me'parādhaḥ śiva śiva śiva bho, śrī mahādeva śambho

Every day I resolve to be better, to handle life with more grace; I resolve to move less by instinct and more by will, with more integrity and grace, but every day I fail in my own eyes. Help me, O Mother, O Lord, to cast off the burden of this perfection that I carry relentlessly. Help me to lay down this burden so that I can be free– free enough to live life according to your will, not mine.

I am gaining a few intermittent glimpses of what it is like to lay down this burden of hurt, guilt, victimization, misunderstanding, and misperception in my life. I see the potential.

As I see the possibilities, a little ray pierces through the dark gloom which has been the life that I have led.
May this ray grow bigger so that I can soak up the light of wisdom, the light of understanding, the light of patience and vigilance: that light which teaches the art of surrender. Oh mother, may I understand that so long as I live my life in accordance to my own desires, I will naturally be apprehensive of the future. O Father, give me the courage and the discrimination to cut the ties that bind with a sword of knowledge and resolution so that the past does not affect the present or cast its shadow on the future. *kṣantavyo me'parādhaḥ śiva śiva śiva bho, śrī mahādeva śambho*

Mother of the Universe, hear my cry. I am a prodigal child, still lost. Rescue me from my own net of helplessness and victimization. Cut the cords that bind with scissors of knowledge and compassion. Instill in me your will rather than my own. *kṣantavyo me'parādhaḥ śiva śiva śiva bho, śrī mahādeva śambho.*

O Mother, O Father, let me dance to the tune of your cosmic beat. Let my feet, faltering at first, find the groove that keeps me within the flow. Let my heart provide the drumbeat for this magnificent journey, leading as I follow. Let your will prevail over mine. O Mother, O Father, wake me from this stupor interspersed with nightmares of my own omissions and commissions, and those of others, that I am not able to forget.

To access the live session, click **HERE** or scan the QR code given below:

OCEANIC AWARENESS

Firm up the posture such that it is conducive for meditation. Bring the head, neck and back into a single line, with the eyes softly closed. The hands should be clasped on the lap with the thumbs touching. Through the closed eyes, the gaze ought to be steady, as though looking at the tip of the nose.

When I assume this posture, the mind automatically gets ready for *dhyānam,* meditation. There is an auto suggestion, an alignment of the mind and the body where the mind responds to the body language of preparing for an inward journey. As I commence this journey, I feel secure. I walk in the footsteps of the ancient sage, *Bhagavān Vyāsa,* who in his compassion has given us the teachings of the Lord *Krishna.* As I begin marking the important steps in this journey, I have nothing to fear, nothing to lose, nothing to gain.

The next step is to connect with the breath. Consciously, I regulate the breath to ensure that the exhalation and inhalation are of equal length. I take long, deep, and as far as possible, silent breaths. In this journey, I notice that watching the breath has the effect of calming the mind down.

The next step along this journey is to keep the external world outside, *sparśān bāhyāṃ bahiḥ kṛtvā.* How does one do this? This becomes clear when I visualize a range of mountains. In relation to these mountains, I find myself a neutral, objective, non-demanding person. I do not wish for the mountains to be any different than how they are. In relation to the mountains, I am happy.

Next on this journey I can visualize the *Gaṅgā,* with her emerald-colored waters flowing. Again the river invokes in me a happy person, free of care. In relation to the river, I am an objective, non-demanding, neutral person, without agenda.

I do not want the river to be a certain way or to flow faster or slower. This is how the mountains are, this is how the river is.

Can I retain this objectivity and dispassion in relation to people? Perhaps with people in general, it is not difficult to do so, so long as one does not have prejudice based on race, gender, and so on. What about people connected to me?

I visualize now the father. Immediately, one can see the difference between the river and the father. The river is outside me, the observer, neutral, objective, and non-demanding. What about the father? Father was and is, outside and also inside, internalized in the form of expectations, regret, guilt, and hurt. Retaining the love and the caring for the father, I can give the father the freedom to be who he is, who he was, *in my perception*. This is how father is, this is how father was. The extent to which I can grant the father the freedom to be however he is or was is the extent to which I am able to free myself from the expectations that he should have been different or that he should be different.

Now I imagine the mother, taking note of the difference between visualizing the mountains and thinking of the mother. The mountains are outside, whereas the mother is both outside and internalized in the form of various emotions. Retaining the caring and the loving for the mother, I grant her the total freedom to be however she is, however she was, *in my perception*. When I do this, I can be free of unrequited expectations and unfulfilled desires in relation to the mother. If there is any residue, I ask *Bhagavān* for help, surrendering any leftover agenda or expectations with regard to the mother and the father at the feet of the Goddess, at the feet of the Lord.

Oṃ īśāya namaḥ, Oṃ īśāya namaḥ, Oṃ īśāya namaḥ, Oṃ īśāya namaḥ, Oṃ īśāya namaḥ,

Next we come to the body. This is how it is. Again, there are two bodies. One is purely external, part of the *jagat,* and two, the body of feelings, full of nonacceptance of so many things about the body that I cannot change.

Oṃ īśāya namaḥ, Oṃ īśāya namaḥ, Oṃ īśāya namaḥ, Oṃ īśāya namaḥ, Oṃ īśāya namaḥ,

I can also observe the mind. Thoughts come, thoughts go. I, the observer, am steady like the windless flame. The mind is an instrument in my hands. An observed mind is a quiet mind. As I watch the mind, I watch the chant, focusing the mind on the chant.

Oṃ, Bhagavān, Īśā, one who is the overlord of all. Unto *Īśā,* my salutations, surrender. Begin the chant (*Oṃ īśāya namaḥ)* mentally, bringing the mind back repeatedly each time it goes away. After a while, I allow the chant to stop. The journey, the one going on the journey, and the destination are one. They are undivided, non-dual, conscious awareness. The meditator, the act of meditation, and the object of meditation are all non-separate from consciousness; awareness itself is morphing, as it were, into the meditator, *dhyātṛ*. When that degree of focus occurs, I can say I am meditating now: *dhyāyati iva,* as-though meditating. When I am distracted, as though away from meditation, it is called *lelāyati iva*. There is no coming and no going in this vast ocean of awareness. I simply am: whole, free, and unfettered. *Oṃ śāntiḥ śāntiḥ śāntiḥ*.

To access the live session, click **HERE** or scan the QR code given below:

CULTIVATING COMPASSION

Soft is the face. Soft are the eyes. Soft is the tongue, sitting heavily in the mouth. Soft are the shoulders, unburdened by cares. Soft is the breath going in, going out. Soft is the gaze on the breath. There is no tension anywhere, just a soft attention, and I see right now there is nothing to do, nowhere to go, nothing to gain, nothing to lose.

I am the meditator, *dhyātṛ*– a simple conscious being. A simple conscious being enjoying my presence, enjoying breathing. I watch as the lungs fill up with air and then empty. I sense the cool air around the nostrils with every inhalation and the slightly warmer air with every exhalation. It is easy to be myself, to just be. Being is my nature and that which is my nature is effortless like breathing. I am a simple conscious being, who is aware, who is breathing.

As I watch my breath, if all manner of thoughts come and crowd the mind, I simply bring back the mind to the breath repeatedly, gently, like a mother dealing with a small child who keeps trying to go on the main road. Just as the mother gently brings the child back to safety of the footpath, I too bring the mind back to softly watch the breath.

Then the next step is consciously gaining objectivity by offloading all that doesn't belong in the head. I visualize the father. This is how he is, this is how he was, *in my perception*. I can see that my perception is not totally objective. Retaining the love and the caring for the father, I can analyze my perception. There are or there might be unrequited feelings, unfulfilled expectations, fear, anger, or feelings of not being treated as I deserve. How to be objective in the face of so many feelings? I take the time to visualize the father as a five year old boy. Innocent, playful, helpless, vulnerable. Here is the father: a small boy. Can I look upon this child with objectivity? Can I look upon this child as I would any other child? I can see the helplessness. I can see that this boy also might have been hurt, wounded emotionally, for no fault of his own.

I can see that he too carried this legacy, the unwanted legacy for pains, hurts, fears which he might have passed on to me unknowingly. Looking at this face of this little boy, I can get some inner space about my own life, my own issues. I can let go. I have the freedom to not participate in carrying this legacy of hurt, distrust, and betrayal. I release this wound. *Oṃ namaḥ Oṃ namaḥ Oṃ namaḥ Oṃ namaḥ Oṃ Oṃ Oṃ*

Now I do the same thing with the mother. First, I visualize the mother. I acknowledge that this is how she is, this is how she was, *in my perception;* I acknowledge my inability to be fully objective. Now I visualize the mother as a five year old child. Innocent, trusting, helpless, vulnerable. Can I look upon this child with objectivity like I would any other child that I might encounter of the same age? Dare I look upon this child with the eyes of compassion, love, kindness? With a little effort, I can see this child too was hurt, betrayed, wounded by elders who did not have the privilege of self-knowledge. They too were children once, unheard and vulnerable, and their elders too.

In acknowledging this *paramparā* of hurt, I can gain some inner space, watching it safely, dispassionately, objectively. Can I see that I have the ability now, the *buddhi* now, to not carry on this legacy of pain, distrust, betrayal, fear, resentment, etc.? Can I see that? Can I make a *saṅkalpa* to drop this legacy that must not be carried forth in my interactions? Can I be free of this burdensome legacy? *Hey, Bhagavan namaste astu.*

Salutations unto you! O Goddess! O Lord! Divine mother and father of the universe, help me to overcome my fears and my tears about my parentage. Help me to let go of all that I am holding on to so tightly. Help me to be in the present. *Oṃ namaḥ Oṃ namaḥ Oṃ namaḥ Oṃ namaḥ Oṃ.*

Now, I look at myself as a small child. A five year old girl or boy. Innocent, eager to please, vulnerable, perhaps even slightly confused about the world around me. Can I gaze at this child with the eyes of kindness and compassion? I visualize myself looking at this child with love.

What might I tell this child? What might I say, when I am face to face with my child-self? Can I see that this child was hurt for no fault of its own? Can I soften the calluses around my heart? Can I let this child into my heart?

Can I give myself a second chance and allow myself to be reparented with the help of the mother and the father of the Universe? Can I soften my heart, my gaze not only towards this child-self, but towards the *jagat* in general?

Can I teach myself how to slow down so that I am not always rushing, running? Can I even entertain the possibility of not being overwhelmed? Can I learn to trust again? Can I learn to let go of hypervigilance? Can I think of letting go of control? Can I also pray to let go of distrust that hardens the heart so that listening to the *śāstra* is more and more effortless and fruitful? Can I just learn to be in my own glory? Can I just learn to be me?

I return to the present, returning to the breathing, watching the chest and the abdomen rise and fall with each breath. I move the fingers and toes, ready to start the day. Ready to be myself, come what may. *Oṃ śāntiḥ śāntiḥ śāntiḥ.*

To access the live session, click **HERE** or scan the QR code given below:

AN APPOINTMENT WITH MYSELF

Throughout the day (in fact, throughout life) there are many, many appointments: at work, online, with friends, with relatives, with doctors, and so on. I keep these appointments faithfully. What about an appointment with myself? What would that look like? What would an appointment with the self look like? Would I even show up, or would I say I do not have the time? How would I greet myself? Would I be excited like seeing an old friend or would I be annoyed? What would I wear for this appointment with the self? Perhaps a better question would be, what kind of masks have to come off as I greet myself?

Firming up the posture, I keep my head, neck and back in a single straight line. My hands are clasped on the lap. The eyes softly close. I watch the body, part by part. I simply watch– I have nothing to do, I have nowhere to go. So I simply watch. The head, neck, and shoulders: this is how they are. I observe the upper back, mid back, lower back, and hips. In the same way, I watch the front of the body, simply watching the chest, stomach, and abdomen.

Now I watch the limbs: the right arm, elbow, forearm, right hand and all the fingers. I bring the same awareness on the left side: left arm, elbow, forearm, left hand and all the fingers. Now I observe the legs: the right thigh, right knee, calf, ankle, and right foot. In the same way I watch left thigh, left knee, calf, ankle, and left foot. Now I watch the body as though I am sitting in front of a full length mirror. This is how the body is. It is a gift, *prasāda*. It helps me move. It takes me places. *Mokṣa-āyatana,* it is a vehicle for *mokṣa*. I can take the time to acknowledge the usefulness of this body. Who is the one acknowledging? The observer, the indweller of the body, a conscious being: *aham*.

Now I watch the breath, just like I watch the body. The breath fills up the lungs and then the lungs are emptied rhythmically, like the flow of mother *Gaṅgā*. I watch the *prāṇa.* Who is this I? P*rāṇī*, the one who wields the *prāṇa. Prāṇa* is inert like the body.

I am the sentient, conscious being. Now I watch the mind. This is how the mind is. When I watch the mind, it becomes tranquil, quiet. When I stray away from watching the mind, I bring back the attention to the mind. I am the master of the mind. I can watch the mind. I can train the mind through the practice of *japa*, which is the definition of meditation: *saguṇabrahmaviṣaya mānasa vyāpāra*. Meditation is a mental activity, whose subject matter is *Bhagavān,* is *Īśvara*. Today we will be using the *mantra Oṃ namaḥ śivāya*. *Śivā,* you are auspicious, blameless, free of guilt and hurt, which is the truth of me, which is my nature, is discovered through the study of Vedanta. *Namaḥ,* salutations unto this *Śivā* who is auspicious, blameless, guiltless, and free of hurt.

Oṃ is a sound of blessing. *Oṃ* is *Bhagavān* with all the attributes of overlordship, power, and so on. *Oṃ* is also *nirguṇa,* free of all attributes, consciousness, *saccidānanda*. We will chant together: loudly, little less loudly, softly, in a whisper, and then silently for a few rounds. *Oṃ namaḥ śivāya*. I allow the chant to stop, reveling in the peace, the *prasāda* of chanting the Lord's name.

An appointment with myself is an appointment with God, *Īśvara*. It is effortless to have an appointment with myself. If that is true, acknowledge that to yourself. It is enjoyable to have an appointment with myself. It is relaxing to be myself. If that is true, you can acknowledge that. *Oṃ śāntiḥ śāntiḥ śāntiḥ*.

To access the live session, click HERE or scan the QR code given below:

ACCEPTANCE OF THE *KARMIC* ORDER

I can take every sound as an invitation to arrive, to return to myself. The temple bells in the background invite me to abide in myself. The occasional bird chirping invites me to be present as does the ticking of the clock, marking time for the timeless one. I take care to assume the posture required for meditation.

The head, back, neck are in a single line. The eyes are softly closed. The hands are clasped on the lap. From here it is easy to embark on the inward journey. The body is the object of my observation, that is very clear, and as I watch the chest gently heaving up and down, I can elongate the breathing. I can observe the breathing. That which is observed is finite. The Truth of the observer is infinite.

Now I begin offloading various impressions gathered based on the primary connections. Visualizing the father, I grant him the freedom to be however he was or is, *in my perception*. Visualizing the mother, I do the same thing, taking the time to acknowledge this is how she is, how she was, *in my own perception*. I grant her the freedom to be whatever she is or was.

I embrace the softness within myself. Soft is the inward gaze directed towards the parentage. Soft is the inward gaze directed towards my own body. This is how it is. When I say this is how it is, it is an acknowledgement of what *is*. What *is*, is *Īśvara*, *Bhagavān*. It is what it is, because it cannot be what it is not. When I want what it is to be what it is not, there is a struggle: conflict, anger, sorrow, pain, fear. What *is* is a law, non-separate from the Lord, non-separate from the Goddess.

What *is*, is the manifestation of *Īśvara* in my life, starting with the mother and father. I certainly did not choose the parents. I could have been born into any family. Why this particular family? Is it an accident, is it a coincidence?

The words "accident", "random incident", and "coincidence" are all names of *Bhagavān,* of *Īśvara*. When we don't understand *Īśvara*, we call it randomness, chance, luck, coincidence, or an accident. Can anything be accidental in this intelligent, orderly *jagat*, which is comprised of a series of orders?

The gravitational force, electrical force, strong force, and the weak force are all orderly in their presentation. Can I see my parentage also as part of the unfolding order of *karma*? Can I see that? My birth order, whether it be as the eldest, youngest, or in the middle, is not an accident. The place of birth too is not an accident. The time and date of birth is not an accident either. The parents to whom I was born was not an accident. What if I look at it in this way? What if I entertain the possibility of a *karmic* order? Does it change my appreciation of my being on this earth? Does it change my rancor and shift my sense of unease with everything in my life? Does it change my insecurity? Does this appreciation of *Īśvara* as non-separate from the *kārmik* order help me to lay down my weapons, resistance, fears, and blocks, and relax in this order? Can this appreciation of the divine order make me into a devotee? When I am a devotee, I can see that any change that needs to happen externally or internally has to come from the source. I have to be in supplication of the source. *tasmai namaḥ tasmai śrīgurumūrtaye namaḥ idaṃ śrīdakṣiṇāmūrtaye*

tasmai–unto that. What is "that?" It is the order, source. *namaḥ*–acknowledgement, surrender, appreciation. When I really understand "it is what it is", starting with this body, this mind, my own background, I am in acceptance. There is a relief, no more fight, no more resistance. Because I understand it cannot be what it is not, I can move on. I can actually take responsibility without blaming others or myself. I can actually see the complex order which has given birth to this background, to this body, to this mind. My reactions to my background are also in order. Anger is in order. Fear is in order.

Resistance is in order. Sorrow is in order. Helplessness and hopelessness too are in order. My regret, which often takes on the forms of the expressions, "why me?" and "why now?", is also in order. The vast psychological order is also *Bhagavān, Īśvara*. The background is what it is. My emotions and my reactions also are what they are. Given this background, this is how the personality is, and it is all also in order.

tasmai namaḥ - unto that, *namaḥ*.

I acknowledge that I have no control over this anger. Now, an interesting thing happens when I look at it in this manner. My anger becomes "this anger". My regret becomes "this regret". My sorrow becomes "this sorrow." Whatever I have referred to as "this", is an object of dispassionate observation.

tasmai namaḥ, tasmai namaḥ, tasmai namaḥ.

This mind filled with these emotions is part of this vast order called *Īśvara*. To have these emotions is natural. It is also natural to be able to override them. That capacity is given just as the emotions are given. The free will to come out of the emotions is given. *namaste astu bhagavan.*

Namaḥ te astu, unto you, the source, the manifestation of this order, my acknowledgement, my appreciation. Oṃ *namaste astu bhagavan viśveśvarāya mahādevāya tryambakāya tripurāntakāya trikāgnikālāya kālāgnirudrāya nīlakaṇṭhāya mṛtyuñjayāya sarveśvarāya sadāśivāya śrīmanmahādevāya namaḥ. tasmai namaḥ, Oṃ namaḥ, tasmai namaḥ, tasmai namaḥ, namaḥ, namaḥ, Oṃ namaḥ, Oṃ namaḥ, Oṃ namaḥ, Oṃ śāntiḥ śāntiḥ śāntiḥ.*

To access the live session, click **HERE** or scan the QR code given below:

Let the māyā cloud reign in the form of the jagat. I am the space-like
consciousness that stands nothing to gain from this rain,
nothing to lose from the saṃsāra deluge.

I AM *SACCIDĀNANDA*

Oṃ namaste astu bhagavanviśveśvarāya mahādevāya tryambakāya tripurāntakāya trikālagnikālāya kālāgnirudrāya nīlakaṇṭhāya mṛtyuñjayāya sarveśvarāya sadāśivāya śrīmanmahādevāya namaḥ.

Check that the posture is conducive for going on an inward journey: the head, neck and back should be in a single, straight line. The hands are clasped on the lap to give stability and the ability to go deep into the meditation. The eyes are softly closed without any wrinkles in the eyelids. The eyeballs are soft, not restless. Soft is the face and the brow. Soft are the cheeks. Soft is the tongue in the mouth. Soft are the teeth, not clenched. Soft are the shoulders, descending downwards softly. Soft is the torso. Soft is the stomach, the abdomen.

Soft is the breath, softly rising and falling like waves on a beach, rhythmic and soft: no tension anywhere, just a small attention. Soft is the *prāṇa vīkṣaṇam.* Softly, the inward gaze is directed to the breath. Soft is the inhalation and soft is the exhalation. I have nothing to prove, and if I find myself hardening in any way, I simply give attention to that body part or the breath and allow it to soften. It is soft all around. Softness is the meditator; there is nothing to defend, nothing to protect. *Oṃ namaḥ Oṃ namaḥ Oṃ namaḥ Oṃ namaḥ Oṃ*

Soft is the hearing that takes place. Now, as I watch the mind, the watcher is soft, kind, and non-judgmental. Soft are the thoughts that fall softly in the mind, like a pleasant drizzle. I am the space-like consciousness that is not affected by the rain of thoughts, even by the deluge of thoughts. When it rains, space does not get wet.

māyā megho jagan nīram varśatu eṣā yathā tathā
cidākāśasya kahāniḥ ko lābha iti sthitiḥ

Let the *māyā* clouds reign in the form of the *jagat*, as the deluge of varied names and forms. I am the space-like consciousness who stands nothing to gain from this rain, and nothing to lose from this deluge. *Māyāśakti*, all knowledge, is compared to a cloud, cloud of knowledge, *prajñānaghanam*. Rain is the *jagat*, starting with my own body-mind complex. In the same way, within this body-mind complex, the cloud that covers my truth, rains the thoughts. Thought-rain happens. Thought *jagat* happens. What is this thought *jagat*? Rain, called the internal *jagat*, is made up of notions, my own notions, my own filters, my own assumptions, prejudices and preferences. The cloud of *ajñāna* rains the *prātibhāsika jagat*. Yet I, *saccidānanda*, do not get drenched. I am immune; I am the immutable, unchanging truth.

When I look upon myself as the cloud, sorrow rises, and anger comes. Even worse is when I think of myself coming under the spell of this rain of sorrow and anger, this rain of terror. I can see how easy it is to look upon myself affected by everything internal, external. Softly, without prejudice, I can let go of this wrong identification. *Oṃ namaḥ Oṃ namaḥ Oṃ namaḥ Oṃ Oṃ Oṃ namaste astu bhagavan Namaḥ, namaḥ te*, unto You O Lord! O Goddess! My surrender, my salutations. *Uddharamām*, help me, the helpless one, extricate myself from the deluge of *saṃsāra*. Repeatedly, I come under its spell due to my wrong thinking because of which I have become touchy, defensive, afflicted by criticism, and judgmental of others and myself. Tearful and fearful, I go about my day like a robot or a zombie, mechanical and afraid to just open the heart due to the fear that it will break. I am needlessly fragile, like a china doll.

Hey Bhagavan, melt this inner world of defensiveness and subjectivity. I do not know how to let this go without basking in your warm and compassionate gaze. Teach me to have compassion towards myself and others. Help me to be strong and not to cave in to the pressure of opinions of the world. Help me to be courageous enough to soften the heart and disarm myself of the weapons of offensiveness and defensiveness.

Help me not to come under the spell of my own subjectivity, notions, fears, and assumptions that shine as though they are real. Rid my heart of the debris of pain and sorrow that I have carried for a long time. Let me be me, untethered and free. Above all, let me see myself as you, as non-separate from you, as shining consciousness: free like space, without a second. Let me be all pervasive all-knowledge. *Oṃ namaḥ Oṃ namaḥ Oṃ namaḥ Oṃ Oṃ Oṃ Oṃ śāntiḥ śāntiḥ śāntiḥ.*

To access the live session, click **HERE** or scan the QR code given below:

HUMAN NATURE IS AN EXTENSION OF NATURE

I see my breathing as an invitation to go inward. I take long, conscious, deep breaths. The breath revitalizes the body, the mind, and the senses. I am the observer that does not need to breathe, sentient and free.

It is not by my inhalation that I am alive, that I am sentient. It is not by exhalation either. I am sentient, self-sentient, *saccidānanda*, not needing to breathe. Whenever the mind goes away, I ask it to come back and watch the breath. Breathing in and breathing out, I am in sync with the whole universe, and from this vantage point of observing the breath, I can help myself to some visualizations of oneness.

Breathing in, I visualize myself as a flower. Breathing out, I feel fresh. Breathing in, I am a flower. Breathing out, I feel fresh. There are many similarities between myself and the flower. The face is like a flower. When it smiles, it's like a flower in bloom. When I encounter the flower in the garden, it is an embodiment of freshness and presence. I do the visualization three more times on my own. Breathing in, I see myself as a flower. Breathing out, I feel fresh. I greet the day with freshness borrowed, so to speak, from the flower.

Hey Bhagavan, let me learn to be in the moment. Let me learn to keep aside the nagging of the past. The past is ever ready to scold me. Free me of its clutches. I want no guilt, no regrets, and no hurts. Take them away. *Hey Govinda! Hey Gopāla!*

Next, I see myself as a mountain. Breathing in, I visualize myself as a mountain. Breathing out, I am strong. I do this on my own for the next few breaths. Breathing in, I visualize myself as a mountain. Breathing out, I am strong.

Hey Bhagavan, remind me of the strength You have given me to face whatever challenges that may come, and rise above them like the mountain. Let the winds of fortune blow. Let the rains of despair come. I stand tall and strong. I have already faced many challenges in my life and survived them. May I know now that I can continue to be strong like the mountain, unmoved by the weather. Let the wind blow, let the rain fall, no matter what happens, I still stand tall. Breathing in, I am a mountain. Breathing out, I am strong, tall, and unbending in the face of difficulties.

Hey *Govinda! Hey Gopāla!*

Next, breathing in, I visualize myself as still water, a placid lake. Breathing out, I reflect the reality exactly how it is. Breathing in, I am still water. Breathing out, I reflect the reality exactly how it is. Like one of those pictures taken by the lake which reflects the trees, the mountains, the sun, exactly how it is. May my *antaḥkaraṇa* be like this lake.

Hey Bhagavan, let the cataract of subjectivity depart from my eyes with the dawn of the knowledge of what *is*. What *is,* is You, *Īśvara.* When I try to make what *is* into what I would like it to be, there is a conflict in the heart. There is confusion, pain, and sorrow. Let the scales of *rāga* and *dveṣa* fall away from my eyes to reveal Your flow, Your vast and beautiful order. When the still water of the *antaḥkaraṇa* is agitated, then my reality is distorted. I have double vision: a vision of division. I am unable to see the truth of myself as everything, everywhere, all the time. I am *sarvātmā.* When the waters of the lake are disturbed within me, there is anger, sorrow, fear, confusion, jealousy, pride, and despair.

I feel far away from You, *Hey Bhagavan*. I feel alienated, alone, and helpless. Help me to be still. Help the mind to be still so that it can discover its own stillness. What *is*, is *Īśvara.* When I am in sync with what *is*, only *Īśvara* prevails. No conflict, no competition. Just the glory of my own being. Breathing in, I am still water. Breathing out, I reflect the reality of what *is*. I do this on my own a few times. *Hey Govinda! Hey Gopāla!*

Breathing in, I visualize myself as space. Breathing out, I am free. There is a vastness within me. There is a vastness in space. No matter what you put in space, it accommodates. It does not feel crowded.

Hey Bhagavan, help me understand this about myself. Let me not succumb to feeling small, bound by obligation, relationships, fears, addictions, sorrow, and despair. Let me see myself as vast unencumbered, ever present, all pervasive *ātman*. Breathing in, I visualize myself as space. Breathing out, I am free. I do this on my own few times.

As a flower, I am fresh. As a mountain, I am strong. As still waters, I am objective. As space, I am free. Nature is my teacher. I can see these things every day and remind myself of my own nature. Human nature is an extension of Nature. *Saccidānanda* is everywhere, in everything. I am never far away from the Truth of myself. Many reminders are there surrounding me to bring me out of any difficult situation. *Hey Govinda! Hey Gopāla! Hey Govinda! Hey Gopāla! Hey Govinda! Hey Gopāla! Oṃ śāntiḥ śāntiḥ śāntiḥ*

To access the live session, click **HERE** or scan the QR code given below:

LETTING GO OF LIMITATIONS

From the standpoint of this body, this mind, and these senses, I feel a number of limitations. Time-wise, space-wise, and object-wise, the body-mind-sense complex is limited, *paricchinnaḥ*. It is physically limited. *Buddhi*-wise it is also limited in what it can remember, recall. The emotions too are limited. The capacity of the sense organs is limited. The organs of action are also limited. The body-mind-sense complex is subject to birth, subject to destruction, and in between, subject to various kinds of limitations.

The I, the meditator, is free of limitations. I know this, yet I find myself repeatedly coming under the spell of various limitations. Repeated twists with the limitations cause doubt, and cause me to have a sense of failure, to suffer from a notion of bondage, and to suffer from guilt, sorrow, fear, and a sense of alienation from the total. *Dhyānam* attempts to bridge this alienation, where I relate to the Total in the form of that which is *Īśvara,* limitless, whole, and free. I am already related to *Īśvara,* but here this relation, this connection is highlighted. *namaste astu Bhagavan Hey Bhagavan, namaḥ te astu.*

Let there be salutations for you. Who is this you? The I that I do not know because my thinking is eclipsed due to wrong identifications. I have to go through You to know the truth of myself as non-separate from You. You embody all that I am, all that I strive to be.

namaḥ te–namaḥ, a word that means many things, including a sense of surrender, and salutations. Why salute anybody? To salute is a form of surrender. What is to be surrendered to? To all that over which I have no power right now: to my background, my parentage, my predilections, my fears, and my core issues, all of which I apparently cannot let go of easily. Unto all that over which I have no power, right now. My background, my parentage, my predilections, my fears, my core issues, which I cannot appear to let go easily. *namaste astu Bhagavan namaḥ,* I let go of my defenses; I am habitually armed to the teeth with all kinds of excuses, fears, and other mechanisms meant to protect all that which does not need protection. They are old and worn out mechanisms of coping which are now useless, defunct. *namaḥ*. I let them go. Even when I cannot let go, I place them symbolically at your feet.

namaste astu Bhagavan namaḥ te, unto You, the limitless one, I surrender the limitations. Who are You? What is your nature? *namaste astu Bhagavan viśveśvarāya, viśveśvarā–viśvasya Īśvara.* You are the one who rules over this universe in the form of various laws over which I have no control. The laws that governs my body, my mind, my senses, my emotions are under your rulership. *Viśva,* universe. *Viśva*, also I, the waking person, the one who is awake, wanting to be awakened to my nature as you, *viśvasya Īśvaraḥ.*

The truth of me is the waker. You are *virāt,* the waking world, connected to me, the individual, the waking person. When I wake up, the world wakes up with me. You are non-separate from the waker and this world, without whom this word cannot exist. *namaḥ te namaste astu bhagavanviśveśvarāya mahādevāya.* The one who is *mahān,* great. In what way are you are great? Greatness in the ability to sustain this world without stress. *Deva is a* self-effulgent being.

O Lord! O Goddess! I am also *deva*. You are *mahādeva* because you do not succumb to the identification with the body-mind complex.

namaste astu bhagavanviśveśvarāya mahādevāya tryambakāya tripurāntakāya. namaḥ te, my surrender, salutations to the one who does not succumb to time. Past, present and future are but your eyes. Unto the one who swallows time. To the timeless one, timelessness personified as *mahādeva,* as *tryambaka, tripurāntaka.* The swallower of time. Time is equal to limitations.

Unto the one who swallows all limitations, unto you I offer my *namaskāra*. Why do I invoke you? I pray for my limitations to be taken away. *Hara hara,* take it away. *Hara hara mahādeva,* take it away, take it away, O self-shining one!

*trikāgnikālāya, kālāgnirudrāya–u*nto the resolver of the three worlds, unto the one who gives *karmaphala.* Not to me but to this body-mind-sense complex, with which I am repeatedly identified. I do not like the *karmaphala,* the fruits of action, I find them hard to accept. I pray for You to neutralize them, to mitigate them, to reduce their intensity, their force, and their frequency.

Oṃ namaste astu bhagavanviśveśvarāya mahādevāya tryambakāya tripurāntakāya trikāgnikālāya kālāgnirudrāya nīlakaṇṭhāya. I bow to the one whose throat is the sky, unto the one who is in the form of the entire universe, *namaḥ* unto you, the blue throated one, vast as the sky. If sky is your throat, formless is your form. *namaste astu bhagavanviśveśvarāya mahādevāya tryambakāya tripurāntakāya trikāgnikālāya kālāgnirudrāya nīlakaṇṭhāya mṛtyuñjayāya*

Salutations to one who has conquered death, endings, which I am afraid of in every given minute: I am fearful of endings, fearful of death. *Namaḥ te,* I surrender this fear at the altar that is you. This fear makes me small; it makes me afraid, insecure, upset. *hara hara mahādevā,* take it away, O Lord! *Oṃ namaste astu bhagavanviśveśvarāya mahādevāya tryambakāya tripurāntakāya trikāgnikālāya kālāgnirudrāya nīlakaṇṭhāya mṛtyuñjayāya sarveśvarāya sadāśivāya*

You are the *Īśvara* of everything, without anything remaining. You are the one who is always a source of auspiciousness. *Śiva*, auspicious. Free me from the inauspicious hold of my own mind, of my own emotions. Let me be free, untethered. May I be the master of my emotions.

Srīmanmahādevāya namaḥ—equipped by *śrīḥ,* the goddess of abundance. May I lose my scarcity mentality, my fears, and my insecurities that make me cling to resources and people. May I have inner abundance. May I speak, act, and think from this inner abundance. Grow my heart to be as large as the galaxies. Let me be objective, non-demanding, and compassionate. Let my heart, with your grace, be able to accommodate the whole universe, at least for today! *Oṃ śāntiḥ śāntiḥ śāntiḥ.*

To access the live session, click **HERE** or scan the QR code given below:

BEING MYSELF IS EFFORTLESS

The seat is firm, yet comfortable. It is not so comfortable that sleep comes, and not so uncomfortable that one has to keep squirming, shifting all the time. The eyes are softly closed. The softly closed eyes are the first indication of wanting to go within. As one continues to practice *dhyana*, meditation, the connection between the posture and the depth that one can go becomes more and more apparent. Assuming the meditative posture itself is an indication for the mind to get ready and to turn from its thoughts, no matter how important it thinks they may be, to do one's bidding. As soon as I assume the posture, the mind is ready for me. It is like any other activity. If I sit at a dining table, the whole body-mind complex is ready to eat. In the same way, this posture is sacred, holy. It's an invitation for the mind to come along. The head, neck, and back are in a single straight line and this posture is maintained throughout the meditation, because when doing *japa,* the head tends to fall forward. The hands are clasped on the lap, and the thumbs are touching gently to give a sense of stability to the posture. The body is like a breathing statue, relaxed.

The next step is to soften from within. The structure for the body recommended in the sixth chapter of the *Bhagavad-Gita* is contrasted by a soft inward demeanor: soft and inviting. How do I get this demeanor? How do I cultivate this disposition for meditation? I watch the body for any signs of tension, a clenching, a hardness. I breathe and soften the shoulders, the jaws, the teeth, the forehead, the whole face, so that I look like the *Buddha* in meditation. I have a soft, calm face. The breathing continues, connecting the outer structure of the body, the statuesque posture contrasted with the softness.

If there are any thoughts that are self-critical, questions about how one meditates, thoughts of inadequacy, or thoughts of self-critique, I gently watch them like a mother lovingly looking at a grumpy child.

This inward gaze of the observer allows the resistance to melt for the blocks to go. Because really speaking, I am being myself in meditation. Being myself is effortless: totally natural to me. I cannot go wrong. I cannot possibly make a mistake. If there are still thoughts that haven't been addressed, I offer them up in prayer.

Hey Bhagavan, however you are, wherever you are, whoever you are, take care of this mind for me. Let me enjoy tranquility. Let this mind be capable of just being itself. Let criticisms directed towards myself and towards the world melt away. Let me be able to offload the people, situations and things that I have internalized, that actually do not belong within. *Hare Rama hare Rama, Rama Rama hare hare*

Take it away. Take away the constant refrain that I am not good enough. Take away the falsehood that I am lacking. Take away the wrong conditioning, hopelessness, disenchantment, anger or fear. Restore a sense of well-being, and the ability to greet the world with curiosity and openness. Do not let the remnants of my childhood rob me of my adulthood. I make peace with my background, because this is how it was, this is how it is. What *is*, is *Īśvara.* Give me the strength to override this background. Once the mind is prepared in this manner, it is capable of *japa,* where the free falling mind is gently trained to do my bidding rather than hijacking me to do its bidding.

Oṃ namaḥ Śivāya–namaḥ, surrender to that which is auspicious. *Śivā,* tranquility. *Śivā,* auspiciousness. What is that which is most auspicious? Myself, *saccidānanda.* What is *Śivā? Saccidānanda.* The *mantra* is carefully placed in the mind and then chanted repeatedly, knowing that there will be distractions that are not the big thing. The job is to bring the mind back each time it runs away, gently and non-judgmentally. Focusing on the spaces between the chants is a way to make sure the mind stays, because the mind tends to leave as soon as it does not have a job to do.

Listen to the spaces between the chants as I chant and pick up the chant mentally as soon as the chanting stops. *Oṃ namaḥ Śivāya Oṃ Oṃ Oṃ*

Let the chant stop for a bit. Ideally the chant should take place in the mind. More often than not, the breath gets involved and one starts to chant along with the breathing. How do I tell if the breath is involved? Pick up the chant again mentally and try to breathe fast with quick, shallow breaths. Did the chant also speed up? If yes, that means the chant is riding on the breath. Do this once again. Speed up the breathing and just watch if the chant has also become fast. After this, return to the normal breath and consciously disengage the chant from the breathing. Breathing happens. Chanting happens in the mind. Continue chanting. There is another technique to deal with the chant. Stop the chant briefly. With the help of some mental arithmetic, I can ensure that the chant comes from the depth of the mind, from a deep place. I think of the number 12. Add 12. Subtract 8. Add 10. Exactly where the answer is received, place the chant and continue.

Once again the chant is stopped briefly. Think of the number 10. Add 15. Multiply by 4. Chant. If this helped deepen the practice that means the exercise was successful. Let the chant stop. Being myself is easy. If that is true, acknowledge that. Being myself is effortless. Being with myself is enjoyable. *Oṃ śāntiḥ śāntiḥ śāntiḥ.*

To access the live session, click **HERE** or scan the QR code given below:

THE LIMITED AND THE LIMITLESS

Any which way one looks at oneself, there is a sense of helplessness and limitation. Body-wise, one is limited and at times helpless. There is only so much that the body is able to do. Pushing it beyond these limits could result in illness, pain, or discomfort. With regard to the *prāṇa* too, one can sense limitations. One can be out of breath at certain points in time. Even the strongest person can be out of breath, pushed beyond a certain threshold of endurance. One is helpless, finite.

Body-wise, also, one is limited. *Prāṇa*-wise, with reference to respiration and all *prānic* functions, one is limited. Mind-wise, also, one is limited. This is easy to see. There is only so much information one can hold, only so much processing the mind is capable of. Memory and recall are limited. In fact, the painful aspects of the past have been deliberately limited, as it were: forgotten and blocked out.

One's emotional capacity is limited as well. There is a threshold of endurance emotionally beyond which one unravels. As for the *ahaṅkāra*, its endurance too is limited. Its identity is based on owning up the body-mind complex, which is also limited, finite. The *ahaṅkāra* is extremely touchy. It does not take long for it to feel insulted, afraid, insecure, or sad. As I ponder on all the limitations and the finitude of the body-mind-sense complex, it is relevant to ask the question, who is this I? For now, we can take the I as a simple conscious being, dwelling in the body, the mind, the senses, and the emotions: *sākṣīn*, the inner witness, *pratyagātman*, the I that obtains in this complex, body-mind complex. Although the observer is free from whatever is observed, one can see that one repeatedly comes under the spell of identifying with the limitations of the body, the mind, the senses, the emotions, and the *ahaṅkāra*.

Oṃ namo bhagavate vāsudevāya. When there is a feeling of helplessness, it is a sign of intelligence to seek help from that source which is responsible for the body-mind complex and its finitude. This seeking is in the form of a prayer. Prayer is an action. The helplessness if it is not acted upon, creates frustration, pain, sorrow. Prayer is an action I can take so that I know I have done my best. *Oṃ namo bhagavate vāsudevāya sarvāṇī bhūtāni adhivasati iti vāsudeva.* Who is this *vāsudeva ?* The one that abides in all *upādhis,* all bodies, all minds. One whose presence is invariable in the midst of everything else which is changing, variable.

Bhagavate–unto this *Bhagavān,* whom I cannot see because it is me, who I cannot connect to because of my own limitations, my blind spots, my resistance, my fears, my distrust. Unrecognized is the presence of this *Bhagavān. To Vāsudeva*–self-effulgent consciousness, that magically abides in all, always– *namaḥ*, salutations.

Oṃ namo bhagavate vāsudevāya is a word of connection. *Namaste–namaḥ te,* I relate to you, the Total, the source of the universe. The one who is present as the law of *karma*, which is responsible for this body, mind, senses, and the *ahaṅkāra. Oṃ namo bhagavate vāsudevaya* Each time this prayer is heard, one can visualize the fears, blocks, resistance melting away, just a bit, bit by bit. *Oṃ namo bhagavate vāsudevāya.* The sad one surrenders to the ocean of *ānanda*, limitless joy. Sadness evaporates. *Oṃ namo bhagavate vāsudevāya.* The angry one relates to that which is an abode of tranquility. *Oṃ namo bhagavate vāsudevāya.* The *mantra* embraces the fearful one. *Oṃ namo bhagavate vāsudevaya* The scattered one relates to the whole. *Oṃ namo bhagavate vāsudevaya.* The one of small knowledge surrenders to the abode of all-knowledge. *Oṃ namo bhagavate vāsudevaya.* The one suffering from ignorance prays for its removal by the source of all knowledge. *Oṃ namo bhagavate vāsudevaya.* I surrender to the abode of compassion.

Hey Bhagavan, teach me to be kind to myself, for only then can I be kind to others. *Oṃ namo bhagavate vāsudevaya.* The subjective one, filled with erroneous notions, surrenders to the total at the altar of objectivity. *Samagraṃ vairāgyam,* total objectivity, dispassion. *Oṃ namo bhagavate vāsudevaya*

The limited one surrenders to the altar that is limitless. Where did the limitations go in this surrender? Where did the tears go? Where did the fears go? Where did ignorance, the small knowledge go? Where did sorrow go? To the same place that the snake went upon the realization that it was a rope. *Oṃ śānti̱ḥ śānti̱ḥ śānti̱ḥ.*

To access the live session, click **HERE** or scan the QR code given below:

THE HUMAN BODY IS *ĪŚVARA'S* MARVEL

Firm up the posture, allowing the posture to be an invitation for the meditation, almost like an auto suggestion. The moment I get into this posture with the head, neck and back in a single line, hands clasped on the lap, eyes softly closed, it's an invitation to go within. The posture tells me that it is okay to go within. Right now, there is nothing to do, nowhere to go, nothing to add, nothing to subtract, nothing to gain, and nothing to lose.

Working with the breath, I first elongate the breath deliberately to make sure that the inhalation and exhalation are of roughly the same length, and as I settle into this practice, I notice that I am more refreshed and recharged.

From here we can have a few rounds of *prāṇāyāma, anuloma viloma,* or alternate nostril breathing. To do that, shut off the right nostril with the thumb, inhale through the left, and then shut off the left nostril with the forefinger, exhaling through the right. Inhale again through the right and then exhale through the left, at your own pace. Continue this practice, making sure that you inhale out of the same nostril out of which you have just exhaled.

If the mind strays, bring it back repeatedly to watch the breathing. The practice of alternate nostril breathing helps to balance the hemispheres of the brain, manage one's emotions, and calm the mind. Watch the breath throughout this practice, which is supposed to be done for six minutes every day in order to get the maximum benefits.

This body is a sacred temple. Using the breath, I can help the body-mind-sense complex to be healthy, to be present, to be ready for the teaching. Next time, when inhaling through the left nostril, I bring the hand back to the lap and breathe normally. I watch how the body and mind feel, and observe.

Watching the body is rewarding because it leads me closer and closer to accepting how it is. I simply watch the body as though I am seated in front of a full length mirror. This is how body is. Many things about this body simply cannot change. Height, general weight, color of skin, predilections towards certain ailments: to all that, *namaḥ*. *Oṃ namaḥ Oṃ namaḥ Oṃ namaḥ*.

The body is how it is, because it is in order. Even though I may want it to be taller, shorter, or have a different skin color, this is how it is: *sthāne,* in order. When I look at it from this standpoint, I see the order not only pervading my body but all bodies in the universe. The eyes are where they should be, the nose is where it should be, the mouth is exactly where it should be. The hands, legs, breathing mechanisms, and *prānic* functions are all exactly how they should be. A miracle is this body, a marvel: *Īśvara's* marvel.

What about the things that do not function? Isn't this disorder? Whatever appears disorderly to me is also included in the order that transcends good, bad, ideal, not ideal, right, and wrong. The order transcends my perceptions. This is how I can appreciate the order that governs this body. Unto that *namaḥ*. Unto that knowledge, the intelligence which makes everything function, *namaḥ*. *Oṃ namaḥ Oṃ namaḥ Oṃ namaḥ*

Watching the mind, again I see it as a marvel: it is always on the move, objectifying various things. It is available for me, a *Bhagavān*-given tool to be able to think, to create, to express happiness which no other life form can express. The mind is a beautiful instrument. I do not know how to make the mind; I can only appreciate it. But, what about the mind that is difficult to train? It is given to sorrow, given to pain, fear, and anxiety. That too is in order: the psychological order. That given a certain background, there will be these kinds of emotions in the mind, is perfectly within the greater order. That is why it is a law.

The ability to come out from under strong emotions is also given. It is also in the order. I see that, and to this vast, infallible order, *namaḥ*. *Oṃ namaḥ*. *Oṃ namaḥ*. *Oṃ namaḥ*. *Oṃ*.

To have the mind more available to me, I can practice *japa,* chanting *Oṃ namaḥ śivāya*. *Śivāya,* unto that which is most auspicious, non-separate from myself: *namaḥ,* salutations, surrender. *Oṃ* is a sound of blessing. Begin the chant mentally, taking care to notice the distractions, bringing the mind back as many times as it takes. Chant. Allow the chant to stop. Watch the spaces between the chants, the next time you pick it up. *Oṃ namaḥ śivāya*. *Oṃ*. *Oṃ*. *Oṃ*. Let the chant stop as we end with the prayer and the desire for the mind to be tranquil, and for me to access this whenever I need it. May all the obstacles to the peaceful mind drop, at least for today! *Oṃ śāntiḥ śāntiḥ śāntiḥ*.

To access the live session, click **HERE** or scan the QR code given below:

RELAXING IN THE ORDER

Oṃ namaste astu bhagavanviśveśvarāya mahādevāya tryambakāya tripurāntakāya trikāgnikālāya kālāgnirudrāya nīlakaṇṭhāya mṛtyuñjayāya sarveśvarāya sadāśivāya śrīmanmahādevāya namaḥ.

We go through the steps of the meditation, the preparatory steps that allow the body-mind-sense assemblage to be a vehicle for the mantra. The seat is comfortable and firm. The eyes are closed softly. The head, neck, and the back are in a single straight line, with the shoulders straight. The gaze is soft and the eyes, underneath closed lids, are pointed towards the tip of the nose. We begin with a few rounds of the practice of internal cleansing called *anuloma viloma prāṇāyāma,* alternate nostril breathing. Close off the right nostril with the thumb and inhale through the left. Close off the left nostril with the forefinger and exhale through the right. Inhale again through the right and exhale through the left. Inhale again through the left nostril, and exhale through the right. Inhaling through the right, continue thus in your own breathing pace. The breath is long, deep and silent.

Six minutes of this practice done every day helps in cleansing the blood and adjusting the immune system in the body. This practice also helps in modulating the blood pressure and balances the left and the right hemispheres of the brain. Adepts can do this practice after several years without the aid of the fingers blocking the nostrils.
Six minutes is what the body takes for the blood to circulate completely. The practice aids in the detoxification of the body and also helps focus the mind in a way that is alert yet relaxed. One can assist this practice with the help of a mantra. Sometimes the *Gāyatrī* is said in conjunction with the alternate nostril breathing. With every inhalation one can say, *Oṃ bhūrbhuvaḥ*. Exhalation, *tatsaviturvareṇyaṃ*. Inhalation, *bhargo devasya dhīmahi*. Exhalation, *dhiyo yo naḥ pracodayāt*.

Oṃ bhūrbhuvaḥ svaḥ, tatsaviturvareṇyaṃ, bhargo devasya dhīmahi, dhiyo yo naḥ pracodayāt.

The above is a collective prayer to the most effulgent Lord, bright as the Sun. It is a prayer for intelligence, a prayer for the capacity to make intelligent choices. The next time you inhale through the left nostril, allow the hand to come down and exhale exhale normally, noticing the subtle shifts in the body-mind-sense assemblage. Perhaps this results in a heightened awareness, a relaxation: an absence of anxiety and a quietened mind.

And then, focusing on the body, begin observing the body part by part. This should be a relaxed observation, an observation that is utterly devoid of judgment. If there is any judgment, I offer it up immediately as a prayer. What I cannot change about this body is out of my hands. I observe the head, neck and shoulders. My gaze is a soft, inward gaze. I observe the head, relaxing it, and then the face, noting any tightness in the jaws, the eyelids, and the facial muscles and allowing any tension to just drop. This is a loose and relaxed observation. I make note of the tension in the neck and shoulders, often connected to stress and carrying mistaken burdens, things that one need not carry. In fact, these are things that one is not really carrying. The shoulders are soothed and relaxed. Relaxation is *Īśvara*.

The front of the body and the chest, I observe. There is no tension in the diaphragm as it fills up with air as the lungs pump the air in and out. There is no tension in the chest, stomach and abdomen. They are relaxed and soft. At the back of the body, the spine is as it were made of magical liquid flowing, elegant, curved, graceful– relaxed. The more I am relaxed, the closer I am to *Īśvara*. The right arm is relaxed. The elbow, forearm, and the right fingers carry no tension. They are just relaxed. The left arm too is at ease, relaxed. The left elbow is relaxed, free of tension. The left forearm, left wrist, left hand and fingers are relaxed, as are the sides of the torso. Right side, relaxed.

Left side, relaxed. Relaxation brings me to *Īśvara*. It is not just a state of the body and mind, It is the Truth of Myself. Now I relax the legs. The right hip is relaxed. The thigh is relaxed. The knee and calf muscle are relaxed. There is no tension, no flexing. The ankle is relaxed. The right foot is relaxed. Now I attend to the left side. The left hip is loose and relaxed. The left thigh is relaxed. The left knee and all the muscles up to the ankle are relaxed. The ankle itself is also relaxed. The left foot is relaxed.

The body is relaxed, ready to receive *Īśvara*. Anxiety takes me away from *Īśvara*. Relaxation brings me to *Īśvara*. All the organization brings me to *Īśvara*. All the organs in the body are relaxed and doing their jobs without any tension. The heart beats without stress. The blood flows without anxiety. There is nowhere to go for the blood. It just flows because that is what it knows how to do. All the muscles in the body that uphold the frame are relaxed.

Connecting now with the breathing, we are also equally relaxed. We take a relaxed inhalation and relaxed exhalation. Breathing in, one can visualize the truth of the words. Breathing in, one can see these words: relaxation brings me close to *Īśvara*. Breathing out, anxiety drives me away. Just visualizing and understanding the truth of these words with every inhalation and every out-breath, every exhalation.

Breathing in, I understand relaxation takes me to *Īśvara*. Breathing out, I understand anxiety drives me away from *Īśvara*. Inhaling, I invite the relaxation, which is the truth of myself. Exhaling, I let go of all stress and anxiety. Inhaling, I abide in *Īśvara,* in relaxation. Exhaling, I let go of all stress. Inhaling, I abide in *Īśvara.* Exhaling, I let go of everything that stops me from abiding in myself. Inhaling, the breathing is fortified and relaxed. Exhaling, I invite the body to cast off the stress. Inhaling, I invite the wholeness, the fluidity, the relaxation – *Īśvara.* Exhaling, I let go of all holding patterns connected to this body. Every inhalation brings me closer and closer to my own presence. Every

exhalation takes me further and further away from that state of hyper-anxiety that I had thought was a way of life. Inhaling, I discover wholeness.
Exhaling, I let go of the fragmented pieces of my life that I am always worried about sewing together. Inhaling, I take on repose, balance and relaxation. Exhaling, I release everything that is the opposite of that. I inhale a state of calmness, *śānti*. I exhale restlessness.

I move now from watching the breathing working with the breath to working with the mind. The subject matter still continues to be *Īśvara* in the form of relaxation. How to discover this *Īśvara*? How to abide in relaxation as a way of abiding in *Īśvara,* when the mind is tied up in knots called in *Saṃskṛta* as the *hṛdayagranthi,* a tangle of the skeins of its own agenda and the threads of misinformation about the truth of itself? The mind is tangled in the web of *saṃsāra*, which is nothing but this becoming-life, characterized by a pressure to be something, a pressure to go and achieve something or the other as a way of staving off the constant dissatisfaction connected to oneself, recognized in the mind.

The mind is on the run and when it runs me, I am on the run too. Watching the mind means disengaging from its commands. The tapestry of the mind is always full of complicated stitches, a multitude of colors often clashing, and the pictures that emerge are those of hopelessness, despair, and distorted versions of the self all woven with skeins dyed in ignorance, which project a picture of myself as a harried being. There is no time to stand, no time to sit, no time to stare, no time to listen to bird song or the swishing of the trees in the breeze. There is the illusion that there is no time to be without doing, that there is only room for doing without being.

The *hṛdayagranthi*, the knot of the heart and the mind is a knotty (and naughty) problem. Entangled in a shadow of its own self, the mind projects the shadows, the shades of myself that bear no resemblance to who I want to be. These are shadows that are larger

than in life loom often, causing fear, stress and strife. Taking the unreal to be real, the mind wanders and becomes a dustbin for all kinds of collected emotions– stress, sorrow, fear, anger, jealousy, desire, frustration, and distrust.
The emotions keep piling and soon it appears that there is no room to hold all of them. One goes through life outburst after outburst; after each outburst, each explosion, each implosion, one goes on for a little while and then again reaches a crisis point.

Disengaging from this cycle, I choose to allow the mind to be what it is. I choose to observe the cycle rather than be a participant, watching *kāma*, desire, do its little jig. "I want, I want, I want." I breathe in again, feeling relaxation. The want dissipates as soon as it is looked at. *Krodha,* anger– whenever a want is thwarted, there is anger. Recognizing that is wisdom. *Lobha*, the insecurity, the needing to hold, I simply watch. *Moha*, delusion– if I am aware of the delusion, that means I am not deluded. *Mada*, pride– from a mistaken sense of accomplishment. *Mātsarya*, intolerance of others' progress, jealousy. the emotions are *Īśvara*. They have their place; they have form and function.

When I watch them with a relaxed mind, I do not allow them to run the show. Just being, just watching, the tapestry unravels. The shadows that are cast are nothing. In fact, they just point to the light, my own light, the light of *Īśvara* that casts the shadows. Bathed in this light, I no longer identify with the shadows. *Hey Bhagavān*, help me to understand myself as the Light of all lights, seeing and being which I no longer have the heart knot. Help me to understand myself as the Light in which the heart knot dissolves. That is the Light of all lights, *jyotiṣām jyotiḥ*.

Allow me to understand anger as a manifestation of you, *Īśvara*. O Lord, desire is nothing but you. Jealousy, mistrust, and fear are nothing but you, a manifestation of you. Help me to recognize them as a manifestation of you. Protect me from being afflicted by them, being afflicted by the sorrows and the stress of *saṃsāra.*

Breathing in, I choose to disengage. Breathing out, I am connected to the Whole.

Breathing in, I choose to disengage from engagement with sorrow. Breathing out, I find that I am the Whole. Clear my heart, O Lord, so I can have a better connection with you, a better view of the Truth of my presence and its glory, its effulgence.

Teach me that you are the *kartā*, the doer. May I learn to practice giving up *kartṛtvam*, doership, every day, as carrying it brings stress and anxiety from carrying the mistaken burden that is already carried by you. Allow me the grace and the wisdom to not be done in by the doings of others. Allow me the luxury of being able to cast off the stress and to understand you as totally devoid of stress. Allow me the grace and the integrity to be responsible around my anger to be able to manage it so that I can give vent to it without hurting others or myself. Kill my greed and pride, *Īśvara*. Let these twin towers within me be fell. Let the inimical forces in the form of desires that lead me astray and run me to the ground be destroyed in the light of your presence, combined with the grace of my surrender.

Let me lose the limitations and learn to gyrate to your rhythms. Let this body and mind be an instrument for you. Let everything that I do be a form of worship, of your glory. Let me learn to flow with your flow. Let all resistance, blockages, fears and stress of trying to upkeep my own flow, of trying to make it bigger than a trickle, be gone. Let me learn to discover how to be free in this flow by flowing freely.

Give me the grace and the courage to process the emotions – *śamā, damā, uparati, titikṣā, śraddhā,* and *samādhānam*. Let the inner resolution, the outer restraints, the ability to let go, forbearance, tolerance, devotion, faith, and a single pointed dedication to my growth, be the six stones with which the path on which I walk is repeatedly paved. Let these six gems be my only ornament. Let me discover through this practice a commodious heart, free of distortion and smallness, a place where I can relax and abide in you. Oṃ *śāntiḥ śāntiḥ śāntiḥ*.

To access the live session, click **HERE** or scan the QR code given below:

Hey Bhagavan, let there be more of you and less of me in me.

TAKE AWAY

I assume the meditative posture. When I assume the posture, the mind gets a message to align itself along with the posture. The mind also falls into place and without being told and starts to watch the breath. In this way, the practice of meditation brings the body and mind into a harmonious relationship. I am in harmony. Everything is how it needs to be.

This indweller of the body-mind-sense complex contemplates, meditating upon the whole, the total. What is the relationship between the individual and the total? Does not the total include the individual? If the total includes the individual, what is the cause of my separateness, feelings of isolation, alienation? What is the cause of fear, of sorrow? Behind all these emotions is a certain helplessness.

When faced with helplessness, it is intelligent to seek help. From whom do I seek help? How do I seek help? The wish to be free of fear, alienation and sorrow can be converted into a prayer. *namaste astu bhagavan. Hey Bhagavan, namaste, namaḥ te*

Salutations unto you! You, that the *Upanishads* say is me, which I am in the process of understanding. I do not even know how to pray. I do not know how to invoke You. I do not know how to be a devotee. On the occasions that I feel strong, when winds of *karma* are blowing my way, I do not feel I need to pray. Only in the helplessness, in times of fear, in times of not being able to change a situation, is the urge to pray is recognized in me. *Hare Rama hare Rama, Rama Rama hare hare.*

O you, the one who takes everything away!
Take away at first my doubt, my diffidence, my hesitation in connecting with you; Take away, take away this doubting mind, replace it with *śraddhā,* trust;
take away the fears, big and small, let me comfortably abide in the all;

take away all the sorrow, let me have no care for tomorrow;
take from my heart the conflict and strife, replace it with the love for life;
take away my subjectivity, which I cannot see, in my glory let me just learn to be;
take away my anger, furious and vast, let me be in peace at last;
take away, take away this alienation by showing me that it's just one more notion;
take away O take away my commitment to *mithyā*
by letting me abide more and more in *satya*;
Take away *tamas* and *rajas*, replace it with *sattva*;
rāgas and *dveṣas* that are strong, please take away,
My desire to better myself, please let that stay;
Spare me from the emotions, the emotional highs and lows,
Teach me to take life as it comes and goes;
Spare me the drama, let me come to know all there is *Rama*;
Take away my pettiness, for it is totally useless;
Let me come out of it, so you please bless;
Take away my regrets, my hurt, my guilt, demolish these mansions that I have built;
Take away tendencies of *adharma*, give me an opportunity to write my *karma*;
Take away the me that is separate from you, let me remain in awareness of you.
Oṃ śāntiḥ śāntiḥ śāntiḥ.

To access the live session, click **HERE** or scan the QR code given below:

LET THERE BE MORE OF YOU, AND LESS OF ME

As I prepare for this inner journey, one thing becomes clear. In assuming of the posture with the head, neck and back in the single straight line, with the eyes softly closed, and the hands clasped on the lap, it becomes clear that this act takes me quickly to the place of the observer, *sākṣīn*. Breathing happens. I simply am, the watcher of the breath. The watcher of all the changes in the body, an effortless witness. It is easy to be a witness; in fact, it is my nature.

The call to meditate puts me in the place of *sākṣin* naturally and effortlessly. Only what I observe keeps changing, not the observer nor the Truth of the observer. When I observe the body, that the body is not me is very clear. *Dehin*, the one who is the indweller, observes the *deha*, that which is *dahanayogya*, fit to be burned at the end of the life. Along with this observation, effortless observing, acceptance also comes in time.

As I observe the body from head to toe, part by part, I acknowledge this is how it is. Acknowledgement is acceptance. It is acceptance of what *is*, is *Īśvara*. There is an immediate relief to not fight against things that cannot be changed, at least immediately. This is how the body is. With the observing, the natural observing, comes this acknowledgement and then the release, the relief.

I am not responsible totally for how this body is. I can make a *saṃkalpa* to take better care of it, to put it on a proper regimen, diet, exercise, etc. But still there are many things about this body I will never be able to change. To those things, *namaḥ;* I surrender. Observation, acknowledgement, and acceptance leads to surrender. I let go and see this body as a manifestation of *Īśvara*, with all its flaws and all its limitations. If I am unable to let go, I pray. *Hey Bhagavan*, this is the body You have given to me. Please let me discover and align myself with its purpose.

Please let me accomplish whatever there is to do. This body is Your body. Tell me what I need to accomplish. Make this body fit for *brahmavidyā*, its ultimate purpose. Reveal to me also its immediate purpose in the world. The more I can let go like this, I let *Īśvara* be. I let go. I let *Īśvara* be.

namaste astu bhagavan

I can do the same thing with my past. When I look upon my past as an expression of the *kārmic* order, there can be a big change if I allow it. I visualize myself as a four year old: small, helpless, and vulnerable. I look upon the four year old with love and compassion. I can even talk to this child, "You are innocent, you have not done anything wrong, you are just a child. And I know that there are many things that you do not understand about yourself, about the caregivers, about the siblings."

namaste astu bhagavan, Oṃ Hey Bhagavan,

The past is not in my hands, yet it leaves a residue on how I look upon the present. The past has come, the past has gone. I can view it not as my past, but as a manifestation of You in the form of a *kārmic* order. I can observe this, I can acknowledge this, and in time as my clarity grows I can accept and surrender to the *kārmic* order. This is a real possibility. But right now, there are more questions than answers. Why did this happen? Why could not I have a different life? Why me? I seek answers to these questions because of my own placement, because of my own shortcomings, *aviveka*, my own blocks, my own resistance. These too are part of the order. My past is the *kārmic* order. My resistance is Your psychological order. Bathe me, O Goddess, in the light of objectivity, *vairāgya*, dispassion, so that I can clearly see more and more that despite everything, I am really free. Unto the *kārmic* order as it awaits my acceptance, I can still say *namaḥ. namaste astu bhagavan.*

You, who are of many forms, have visited me as the *kārmic* order, ever unfolding. A helpless person I am, when faced with this mega order. Give me the grace to surrender. Give me the integrity to continue to follow *dharma* despite setbacks. *Oṃ namaste astu bhagavan.*

I did not make my mind. I have not made my senses. I am not even responsible for my thoughts; I know not from where they come. This mind with all its issues, doubts, fears, and tears, I place at your feet. *namaste astu bhagavan. hara hara,* take it away.

My core issues make sense. They have a purpose, or they had a purpose. Perhaps they were a coping mechanism which has left a residue in how I see and interact with the world. Enlighten me to the fact that I no longer need these mechanisms, defensiveness, offensiveness, avoidance, withdrawal, resistance, or blocks. These are all the *āyudhā,* the implements or the weapons of the innocent child, who is left to face the world without any help. Now I have help. I have You. O Lord! O Goddess! I have *Vedānta.* I have *ātma anugraḥ.* I permit myself to grow out of these reactions. *Oṃ namaste astu bhagavan*

What would it look like if these weapons of the past were just dropped? With the Lord's grace, maybe I can let go of them, one by one, if not all at once. Maybe I can be less defensive, less offensive, less guarded, less anxious, less worried about the future. Maybe I can let go a little bit at a time, of the resistance. Maybe I can let go of the tendency to self-sabotage. Maybe I can let go of the tendency to get ahead of myself. Maybe I can let go of constantly interrogating, questioning myself and others. Maybe I can let go of the deep sorrow to which I appear to be attached. Maybe I can let go of the fear that is lurking in every corner. The mind is You. The psychological order is You. I give back unto You what is already Yours, but which I had mistakenly appropriated as mine. *Namaste astu bhagavan. Oṃ Oṃ Oṃ.* Teach me to see this whole universe as a manifestation of You, starting with my own body, my mind and senses.

Teach me to invite You more and more into my life. Teach me to let go of distrust. Replace it with *śraddhā*, trust in that which is infallible. Let the distrust of the childhood be replaced by the trust in the infallible as the mother and father of the universe. Let there be less and less of me. Let You preponderate. Let there be more and more of You.

Oṃ śāntiḥ śāntiḥ śāntiḥ.

To access the live session, click **HERE** or scan the QR code given below:

DARŚAN IS ABIDANCE IN THE SELF

Accept an invitation to go within, carving out a time for myself from the busy days ahead. The body forms itself into the posture for meditation, yet is relaxed. I soften the face: soft is the brow, soft are the eyes. The eyelids are softly closing. Soft are the jaws. Soft is the tongue between the teeth. Soft are the shoulders moving back and away from the ears. Soft are the thoughts that softly fall into the mind. There is nowhere to go right now. There is nothing to achieve, to gain or to lose. Nothing. No pressure. There is just a general softness in the demeanor. As I look at my breath, it is also soft: soft, silent, and deep. There is no rush and no push, just elongating the breath softly to ensure that the exhalation and the inhalation are of the same length.

I practice *deha vīkṣaṇa*, looking upon this body as a temple, *deho devālaya proktā*. The head is the *śikhā*, the spire of the temple. I visualize the heart as the sanctum sanctorum, *garbhagraha*. *Jīvo deva sanātana:* the *jīva*, the individual I, is the indweller of this temple, eternal and always there. I visualize *Bhagavān,* present in the chest cavity occupying this temple. This *Bhagavān* can have any name, any form. *Aṅguṣṭhamātraḥ puruṣo madhya ātmani tiṣṭhati, īśāno bhūtabhavyasya na tato vijugupsate, etadvaitat.*

The *Bhagavān* that is the indweller of this body, I give it a name, a form right now. *Aṅguṣṭhamātraḥ,* this *Bhagavān,* is like the thumb, not so much in size, but in terms of its functionality of giving the hand its capabilities. Without the presence of the thumb, the fingers are of no use. Without the presence of this indweller, this body-mind-sense complex is of no use. *Madhye ātmani tiṣṭhati,* this *puruṣa,* this *Bhagavān,* resides in the heart. *Īśāna, Īśvara* of the past and the present and the future, timeless *Bhagavān* residing in this time bound body, as it were. *Deho devālaya proktā, jīvo deva sanātana.*

Everything I do, every action, every word, every thought, is blessed by *Bhagavān* in the heart. Why is it so hard to connect with this *Bhagavān* during the rest of the day? *Tyajeta ajñānam nirmālyam:* my own *ajñānam* is likened to old dried flowers that were once fresh and adorning *Bhagavān,* but right now they are just obfuscating the vision. I pray for this *ajñana* to be removed by Bhagavan, because of whose grace I can have darshan. I can abide in this knowledge. Abidance indeed is *darshan*.

Oṃ īśāya namaḥ, Oṃ īśāyai namaḥ I continue with this chant silently. *Oṃ īśāya namaḥ, Oṃ īśāyai namaḥ* Continue the chant. *Oṃ īśāya namaḥ, Oṃ īśāyai namaḥ Oṃ īśāya namaḥ, Oṃ īśāyai namaḥ*. I allow the chant to stop. *Hey Bhagavan, hey Bhagavate*, let me ever be aware of your presence in my heart, in this body-temple. Guide my *buddhi*, making it free of impulsivity and reactivity. Let the compassion that is You pervade my mind, my *buddhi*. Let Your presence always remind me that the Truth of me is an objective, non-demanding, compassionate, non-judgmental person. Bless me to be this every day. Bless me, above all, to be this today. *Oṃ śāntiḥ śāntiḥ śāntiḥ*.

To access the live session, click **HERE** or scan the QR code given below:

MĀNASA PŪJĀ: MENTAL WORSHIP

Oṃ namaste astu bhagavanviśveśvarāya mahādevāya tryambakāya tripurāntakāya trikāgnikālāya kālāgnirudrāya nīlakaṇṭhāya mṛtyuñjayāya sarveśvarāya sadāśivāya śrīmanmahādevāya namaḥ. Firming up the posture and watching the breathing, visualize the chest cavity as a temple, inviting *iṣṭa devatā, Bhagavān,* in any form that you please, that you can connect to. Invite this *Bhagavān* to abide in the temple of the heart. *Aṃguṣṭhamātraḥ puruṣo madhya ātmani tiṣṭhati, īśāno bhūtabhavyasya na tato vijugupsate, etadvaitat.* I visualize a small version of this *Bhagavān* in the chest cavity, inviting this *Bhagavān* to come and abide in the heart. Of course *Bhagavān* already abides in the heart, but this visualization highlights that through *mānasa pūjā.*
āvāhito bhava, sthāpito bhava, avakunthito bhava, prasīda prasīda.

Āsanam, offering a place to sit, comes first. Since it is *mānasa pūjā,* I can be very lavish. A silk or velvet *āsanam* with a gold border and so on can be visualized.

Arghayaṃ, offering water to drink and water to wash the feet, is next. I visualize collecting water from all the holy rivers for *snānam,* bathing *Bhagavān, Bhagavatī* sitting in the right side of the heart.

Bhagavan is bathed not just with water, but with milk *abhiṣeka,* yogurt *abhiṣeka,* fruit salad *abhiṣeka* with honey, fruit juice *abhiṣeka,* and then followed by holy *dravyas, candanam:* sandalwood paste *abhiṣeka, vibhūti* water *abhiṣeka*. And as these various materials are being anointed, I visualize the heart being cleansed of *rāga-dveṣa.* With each *abhiṣeka*, I am cleansed of strong preferences, prejudices.

Like the outside *abhiṣeka* in the form of the rain cleans the atmosphere, cleans away the dust, and clears away all the toxins and the pollution, so too the inside *abhiṣeka* clears away inner toxins in the form of pains, sorrows, anger, fear, jealousy and self-sabotage.

Outside raindrops are the *abhiṣeka* within, and the noise of the thunder is the percussion to accompany this inner *pūjā*. The rain and the thunder make nice music to accompany this holy sacred inner *pūjā*. Finishing up the *abhiṣeka* within, I wipe *Bhagavān, Bhagavatī* with the softest of cloths, placing them again on a new *āsana,* made of gold, studded with diamonds and other precious gems. I dress *Bhagavān, Bhagavatī* with the best and richest of clothes with gold borders, decorated with precious gems.

With *ābharaṇa,* all kinds of jewels, from head to toe I can decorate *Bhagavān* to the music of the rain and the drum beat of the thunder. Head ornaments, a crown, earrings, a necklace, armbands, bracelets, rings, a waistband, anklets... all this I offer lovingly and with leisure along with the prayer, may these ornaments I offer adorn me in the form of the head ornament of *viveka,* the earrings of *vairagya, mumukṣutva,* the necklace studded with the gems of *śamā, damā,* and the other virtues. Let me wear the bracelets of *jijñāsā, the* desire for knowledge. Let me wear the anklets of responsible *karma,* being mindful of how I move, where I go, what I say, what I choose not to say. I offer to *Bhagavān, Bhagavatī* the *Yajñopavīta,* a sacred thread with a prayer that this thread may symbolize for me an unshakable commitment to these teachings. May I never swerve from them.

I offer d*hūpa,* the incense stick. The glowing incense stick moves around the form of the Lord within. That glow is myself, the self-sufficient, self-standing, *ātman.* When I stop moving the incense stick, all there is, is this glow. Let the moving incense stick symbolize the *jagat:* consciousness plus the *jagat.* The non-moving incense stick may symbolize pure consciousness. *Hey Bhagavān, hey Bhagavatī,* may I know this. The temple bells ring in the distance, inviting me to abide the Truth of myself a little deeper.

Bring back the mind if it has gone away. The temple bells reiterate my decision to commit to the Truth of myself in the form of this *mānasa pūjā*. Let the fragrance of this knowledge, like the incense, spread far and wide in my prayer. *Dhūpam, dīpam,* and *ghīlap* waved in front of *Bhagavān, Bhagavatī* remind me to nourish myself so that even though I am in this finite body-mind-sense complex, I can take care of it and make it a vehicle for *mokṣa.* Let the lamp burning brightly be my desire for this knowledge. May my *buddhi* be focused and wonderful.

Next, *naivedyam* is prepared. All the dishes from all parts of the world I can conjure up mentally and offer. Let this *naivedyam* metaphorically signify the offering of my *ahaṅkāra* to You. I surrender. I no longer resist. I offer my desires. I offer up my actions. I offer the results of action unto You. *Oṃ praṇāya svāhāḥ, Oṃ apānāya svāhāḥ, Oṃ samānāya svāhāḥ, Oṃ udānāya svāhāḥ, Oṃ vyānāya svāhāḥ, Oṃ brahmaṇe svāhā.* Now for the much awaited moment: the *āratī*. I light the camphor lamp, its fragrance wafting to my nostrils. I shine up *Bhagavān* in the heart from head to toe, revealing the truth of myself.
Na tatra sūryo bhāti, there is where the sun does not shine.
na candratārakaṃ, neither does the moon, nor the stars.
nemā vidyuto bhānti, these lightnings also do not light up Truth.
kuto'yamagniḥ, what to talk of this miserable light that I offer You.
tameva bhāntamanubhāti sarvaṃ, in whose light all lights are revealed, in whose presence, the sun is revealed, all other sources of light are revealed. When this light is there, every other light is seen.
tasya bhāsā sarvamidaṃ vibhāti, this light shines up everything. Light of *ātman*. Light of knowledge. Everything shines after, *anubhāti.*

This light only, *bhāti.* May the camphor lamp, signifying the light of the *śāstra* entering my heart, illumining *Bhagavān* within, help me to recognize the truth of myself.

I sit down to just watch this magical *pūjā*, internal *pūjā*. There is nothing to want, nothing to gain, nothing to lose, nothing to protect, nothing to achieve, nothing to keep. The fruits and the flowers at the altar symbolize the dedication of my *karmaphala*, the results of action, to *Bhagavān*. Save me from being too attached to the results of my action; hey *bhagvan, hara hara*, take it away, take it away. In the next step, *kṣamāpanā,* I acknowledge the many mistakes I may have done in the course of this offering. *Kṣantavyo me'parādhaḥ śiva śiva śiva bho śrīmahādeva śambho.* There are so many difficulties, so many mistakes. Not only in this *pūjā,* but in life. Who else can overlook these? Who else can forgive these other than You? Who else can absolve me of my guilt, of my hurt? You alone I turn to. You alone can help.

I allow *Bhagavān* to be established in the heart with a parting prayer. Let me never lose sight of You within. Let You be always accessible to me, as me, in me. Let me go with the flow. Let there be more and more of You, less and less of me. More objectivity, less subjectivity. More acceptance, fewer complaints. *Oṃ śāntiḥ śāntiḥ śāntiḥ.*

To access the live session, click **HERE** or scan the QR code given below:

I AM COMFORTABLE BEING MYSELF

The seat is firm, yet comfortable. I guide myself through the various steps of the meditation, starting with the posture. The head, neck and back fall into a single straight line. The hands clasped on the lap. I utilize *prāṇa vikṣaṇam* to come back to the body, to the place of the neutral observer, *sākṣīn.*

I take the time to visualize the mother. I acknowledge that this is how she is, she was, *in my perception*. Retaining the care and the love for the mother, one lets go by giving the mother the freedom to be who she was, who she is. In so doing, one finds the freedom from having expectations that could not be fulfilled, that cannot be fulfilled.

Hey Govinda! Hey Gopāla!

Towards the father I do the same thing on my own, visualizing him and granting him the freedom to be however he is, however he was. I am feeling free of the burden of unrequited expectations.

hare Rama hare Rama, Rama Rama hare hare

I do the same thing with my body, *śarīra vikṣaṇam.* This is how the body is. Visualizing the body from head to toe, I become objective.

sparśān bāhyāṃ bahiḥ kṛtvā

I ensure that I am keeping the external world outside, a very crucial step in the meditation. Many things about the parents could not change, cannot change. Many things about the body could not change, cannot change. If there are still expectations or wishes that will not go away, I convert them into prayer.

Namaste astu bhagavan. An unacted-upon wish becomes a cause for frustration. Prayer is an action which transforms the desire into surrender. *Namaste astu bhagavan.*

I let go of all the things that I cannot change, that I cannot control. I let go. I visualize the *raga-dveṣas* and the inability to let them go evaporating like water on a hot day. When I let go, there is sense of less burden and I can heave a sigh of relief. I am part of the order, this body-mind-sense complex is part of the order, which is a manifestation of *Īśvara.* My talents and my shortcomings are not an accident. My body is not a mistake. There is deliberation and purposefulness in the universe that also includes my body, my mind, my senses. I am tired of this tug of war of trying to manufacture *karmaphala.* I let go, and whatever fear comes during letting go, I give that to you. *Namaste astu bhagavan.*

I move now to watch the mind. Here too there are lots of opportunities to let go. A thought comes; the thought is gone. I am that unchanging *ātman*, the observer of the thoughts. I take my time to watch the mind.

Whenever the attention strays from the mind, I bring it back to watch the mind. In this mind, I place the *mantra*. Today we can use the mantra *Oṃ namaḥ śivāya.* We will begin chanting together loudly, then a little less loudly, then softly and then silently for a few rounds.

Allow the chant to drop. See if you are a little lighter, a little more comfortable living in this body, in this mind, with these senses. If so, you can acknowledge that to yourself: "I am comfortable being myself. Right now, I am comfortable being myself. This means I do not require any comforting from others, at least for today. Perhaps I can even be a source of comfort to others." *Oṃ śāntiḥ śāntiḥ śāntiḥ*

To access the live session, click **HERE** or scan the QR code code given below:

Hey Bhagavan, grant me the dispassion to separate myself from my deep rooted patterns,, behaviors, and emotions. Let me see these as a legacy that I do not need to reproduce any longer. Help me to let go.

ABIDING IN *ĪŚVARA*

I let the posture that I assume to help me meditate be an invitation to go within. Enjoying a happy anticipation of being myself, being with myself, I soften the brows, the eyelids, and the jaws. Soft is the face, like the statues of the *Buddha* in meditation. Soft is the tongue lying between the rows of the teeth. Soft is the belly, moving in and out along with the breath, which is also soft.

Soft is my disposition towards the external world of objects. I visualize a range of mountains. In relation to these mountains, I find myself to be an appreciative, non-demanding, objective, accommodative person. I do not have an agenda for how the mountains should be, or for that matter, should not be. When I look upon the river, I experience the same thing. What greets the river is an appreciative, non-demanding, objective, accommodative person. Soft is my disposition, my temperament as I greet the river, the mountains and many other things in the universe – flowers, trees, and so on.

Can I retain this disposition when I look at people? Perhaps I can toward people in general, as long as I do not carry bias or prejudice based on race, ethnicity, or gender. But, when we talk of the people close to me, there is a difference. There is a difference between visualizing the mountain and visualizing the mother. Why is there this difference? The mountain is outside, but the mother is both inside and outside. How to keep what is outside, outside? How to regain my appreciative, non-demanding, objective, accommodative, and cheerful disposition with regard to the mother?

I visualize the mother as a child; perhaps she is three or four. When I look at this child, I can see that it can do no wrong. She is small, defenseless, and vulnerable. This is how the mother once was. What kind of difficulties might she have endured growing up? What kind of hurts might she have inherited from the families?

But right now, as I look at the face of this child, it is easy to see myself as an appreciative, non-demanding, compassionate, objective person. It is, what it is. Hey *Bhagavan,* make me emotionally strong so that my threshold for acceptance and accommodation, and perhaps even forgiveness, increases.

For the father, I do the same thing, imagining a three or four year old boy. This child has no power to hurt. He is small, defenseless, and vulnerable. As I gaze upon the face of this child, it is easy to be an appreciative, non-demanding, objective and accommodative person.

I can do the same thing with myself. I look upon myself as a toddler, a three or four year old child. As I gaze into the eyes of this child, I can see that it is perfect. It does not have to do anything to be loved. It is lovable. I can tell this child that, in so many words. I can separate the child from the grown up, from the issues that I carry from my behavior, my conduct, and my overall reactivity. My nature is like that of the child: happy and spontaneous, bearing no ill-will, grudges, or resentment.

I can carry myself with trust, trusting easily, being appreciative. It is my nature to greet the world cheerfully. It is my nature to be happy with whatever there is.

Hey Bhagavan, grant me the dispassion, the objectivity to separate myself from my deep rooted patterns, my beliefs, my notions, my behavior, my emotions. Let me see these as a legacy of growing up that I do not need to reproduce. Help me to let go.

Let me regain my all-around well-being, physically, mentally, and emotionally. Give me courage to let go of old coping mechanisms; they are defenses that are no longer useful. Increase for me the threshold of my tolerance.

Teach me to live in harmony with everything and everybody. Let me learn to be open and more trusting. Remove all of my doubts and my hesitation. Teach me to let go. *Hey Bhagavan, namaste astu*. I cannot do this without your help.

As time goes on, let there be more and more of you pervading me. May there be more and more of *Īśvara,* and less and less of the complaining me. More *Īśvara* means more appreciation. More *Īśvara* in me, as me, begets more cheerfulness. More *Īśvara* means more objectivity. More *Īśvara* means fewer complaints. More *Īśvara* leads to more accommodation. More *Īśvara* begets less suspiciousness. This is what I am. This is what I want to discover. *Oṃ śāntiḥ śāntiḥ śāntiḥ*.

To access the live session, click **HERE** or scan the QR code given below:

Oṃ namaste astu bhagavanviśveśvarāya mahādevāya tryambakāya tripurāntakāya trikāgnikālāya kālāgnirudrāya nīlakaṇṭhāya mṛtyuñjayāya sarveśvarāya sadāśivāya śrīmanmahādevāya namaḥ

namaḥ te astu. Whatever exists in my life over which I have no control, to those things that I cannot overcome: unto that, *namaḥ.* The word *namaḥ* is not an expression of defeat. I learn to see it as an expression of wisdom. Wisdom is in being able to differentiate between what I can and cannot change, at least for right now.

namaste astu bhagavan

There is not just surrender in the word *namaḥ,* but also in *jñānam,* wisdom. There are many things I cannot change, like even this body: the kind of challenges it may have, intolerance of certain foods, and the poor reaction to certain types of climate are all beyond my control. When I say to all this, *namaḥ te astu,* I am not giving up. I am in acceptance. There is a big difference. I choose my battles carefully. Where is it that I can have a sphere of influence? What is it that I can change? What is it that I cannot? When I am in acceptance, I am in the flow of *Bhagavān, Īśvara,* the universal intelligence, the universal flow. Suddenly things are calm and I am at peace.

Next, I make peace with my background. This is how the mother was or is, how the father was or is, *in my perception*. Retaining the care for them, I am able to see that this relationship includes my expectations. Here too, I can say *namaste astu, namaḥ* to those expectations that simply won't go away, even in the light of the fact that that they cannot be, or could not be, fulfilled. *Namaḥ* to this mind of the child holding on to these expectations.

namaste astu bhagavan

I accept that there are expectations. I accept that they haven't been fulfilled. I visualize surrendering these expectations over which I have no control at the altar that is *Bhagavān*. What *is Bhagavān?* Vast enough to include my unfulfilled expectations. I can pray for clarity. I can pray for wisdom. I can pray for the ability to grow out of these needs, these expectations. I am one step closer to making peace with my background. This is how my childhood was.

I visualize myself as a small child of four years old: small, vulnerable, and innocent. Perhaps at that age I laughed a lot and played and jumped, or perhaps I was a serious child. Nonetheless I greeted the world with enthusiasm, curiosity, spontaneity, and creativity. Now, *hey Bhagavan,* my life is full of inhibitions, fear of wrongdoing, pressure to not make mistakes, and pressure to be a certain way at a certain time.

I go back to this child –small, innocent, spontaneous, unafraid– and look upon them before they took all the burdens of the world onto the shoulders. I look upon this child as a teacher. I can even ask this child, what can you teach me about letting go, about living in joy, about resilience? Teach me to pick myself up each time I fall. Teach me to let go of grudges and resentments. The child Self is *Bhagavān.*

namaste astu bhagavan

To all that transpired between the life of the child and the life of the adult now, unto all those events, situations, people, and encounters: *namaḥ*. They have formed me. They have taught me a few things. All my challenges and experiences in life are not wasted, and to each thing that has helped me grow, *namaḥ*.

namaste astu bhagavan

All the challenges, disappointments, fears, and loss of trust have been the rungs on the ladder of emotional growth. When I look upon the sorrows and difficulties in my life from this standpoint, I can thank them for making me what I am now. Still I can trust. Still I can open the heart. Still I can be a loving being.

namaste astu Bhagavan

To those aspects that are not very helpful, unto them also *namaḥ*. I see the old coping mechanisms that are of no use at this point in my life. I can let them go.

namaste astu Bhagavan

To all defenses and offenses, *namaḥ*. To old ways of trying to protect myself from real or imaginary threats, *namaḥ*. To old fears that keep me bottled up, *namaḥ*. To old sorrows that I need not reproduce, *namaḥ, namaḥ, namaḥ*. It is old baggage that has outlived its usage.

namaste astu bhagavan

I pray for all these to go. All that does not serve me now. O *Bhagavan,* You know what they are; take them away. *hara hara mahādeva. hare Rama hare Rama, Rama Rama hare hare*

To the old feelings of helplessness which have no role to play now, *namaḥ*. To the feelings of victimization, and the notion that I am a helpless being, *namaḥ*. Give me the blessing of clarity, of the *buddhi.* Give me the blessing of *vairagya,* objectivity, where I can see everything as not targeting me. Let there be more and more of *Bhagavān* pervading this body, this mind, and these senses. More *Bhagavān* means more objectivity, more peace, more creativity, more spontaneity. Let there be less and less of the fearful, tearful one. Let there be one flow. Let me be always in this flow.

namaste astu bhagavan. Oṃ śāntiḥ śāntiḥ śāntiḥ.

To access the live session, click **HERE** or scan the QR code given below:

May I learn to see all challenges, fears, and losses as rungs on the ladder of emotional maturity. May they bring me clarity and peace.

This body is how it is, because it is in order... When I look at it from this standpoint, I see the order not only pervading my body but all bodies in the universe. This body, is a miracle; this body is Iśvara's marvel.

SECTION II

CONTEMPLATION *(NIDIDHYĀSANA)*

I am an investor in
the real estate of the heart
my home is called *'Om'*
viveka and *vairāgya*
graceful drapes billow
in the *brahmavidyā*-breeze
the *śama-dama* vacuum
traps the *saṃsāra*-gloom
śraddhā, the centerpiece
is where conversations
on freedom flow
with this as the interior decor
mokṣa dances at the door.

I appreciate Īśvara in the form of the respiratory order. When I look at Īśvara in this manner, it is no longer my breathing, my prāṇa. It is a law that governs the breathing of all beings I am one with everything that breathes.

DISCOVERING THE *SĀKṢIN* (WITNESS)

Namaste astu bhagavanviśveśvarāya mahādevāya tryambakāya tripurāntakāya trikāgnikālāya kālāgnirudrāya nīlakaṇṭhāya mṛtyuñjayāya sarveśvarāya sadāśivāya śrīmanmahādevāya namaḥ

The seat is firm, yet comfortable. It is not so comfortable that sleep comes, and not so uncomfortable that one cannot maintain the posture for the duration of the meditation. Assuming the recommended posture with the head, neck and back are in a single straight line, I hold it mindfully. This is important because as one starts to meditate, the head can droop. There are no wrinkles in the eyelids, no effort, and no tension. The eyeballs are not restless in the eye sockets, but are looking forward as though focused on the tip of the nose.

Then I focus on my breathing, without altering the breathing. I just do *prāṇa vīkṣaṇa:* I watch the breath go in and out, making sure that the inhalation and exhalation are roughly the same length.

These detailed instructions are there given to us by Lord *Krishna* in the *Bhagavad-Gita*. If the mind strays from watching the breath, I gently bring back the mind to do its job. When I watch the breath, the mind falls in place. It becomes more present, more tranquil.

This instruction to keep the outside world outside seems a bit peculiar. The so-called outside world is already outside. How can I keep what is already outside, outside? I visualize a range of mountains. In relation to these mountains, I find that I am an objective, non-demanding, accommodative, and non-complaining person. I do not wish for the mountains to be of a particular shape or the size.

In other words, I am happy with the way they are. Next I visualize a river. This is how river is. Again in relation to the river, I find myself to be a relaxed person, a stress free person, an objective person. I am non-demanding and free.

Now, I visualize the mother. Immediately one can see that there is a difference between the mountain and the mother. The mountain range is external; the mother is also external, but while the river remains "outside," the mother is internalized in the form of anxiety or unmet expectations. This is why *Bhagavān* Krishna says to keep the external world outside.

How is this accomplished? I visualize the mother. This is how she was, this is how she is, in my perception. It's important to add this phrase "in my perception". I could be right, but I need not be right. I take the time to grant the mother the freedom to be however she was, however she is. The more I am able to do this, the more I am able to free myself from the expectation that she should have been different, that she should be different. Retaining the love and care for the mother, I grant her the freedom to be however she was, however she is.

Hare Rama hare Rama, Rama Rama hare, hare

With regard to the father, I do the same thing. This is how father was, father is, in my perception. Retaining the love and care for the father, I grant him the freedom to be whoever he was, he is, however he was, he is. If I am successful in this exercise, then I have offloaded the subjective father, subjective mother, sitting in my head in the form of various notions, expectations and anxieties.

Oṃ namaḥ, Oṃ namaḥ, Oṃ namaḥ. Oṃ. Oṃ. Oṃ.

Shifting the attention to the body, again I can ask the question– is it external or internal? I observe the body as though I am sitting in front of a full length mirror.

This is how the body is. There are many things about this body that I cannot change: the height, the general range of weight, the color of the skin, a predilection to certain ailments, and so on. This is how the body is. This is how the body is. I let it be, however it is. There are many things about this body I would like to change. But right now it does not seem possible, despite trying very hard.

I convert this wish into a prayer. When a wish is not acted upon, it causes frustration. Prayer is an action. *Hey Bhagavan*, grant me the ability to change the things in this life that I can, grant me the acceptance of all the things right now that cannot be changed, grant me the wisdom to know the difference. *Oṃ namaḥ, Oṃ namaḥ, Oṃ namaḥ. Oṃ. Oṃ. Oṃ.*

I now observe the mind. A watched mind is a quiet mind. This is how the mind is. The mind is momentary. The watcher of the mind is permanent, infinite. The mind, is an object in my awareness. The observer is the true I, awareness itself, awareness incarnate.

Hare Rama hare Rama, Rama Rama hare, hare.

Hearing takes place. I simply am. I am the watcher, the observer. I am present. I am the *nitya-ātman*, the Eternal "I." I am the *śuddḥa-ātman, the* pure "I," free of blemishes, free of omissions, commissions, guilt, or hurt. I am the *buddha ātman;* the nature of the observer is the shining, knowing being, the All-knowledge "I." I am the *mukta-ātman,* ever free. There is no bondage, no notion of being trapped, bound, or afraid.

The *nitya, śuddḥa, buddha, mukta, ātman* - this is my nature, my *svarūpa*. The body, the mind, and the senses are all objects of my observation. I am a *sākṣīn*: the free observer, pure conscious awareness. *Hare Rama hare Rama, Rama Rama hare, hare*

The body: an object. The mind: an object. The senses: objects. Anything that is an object is *jaḍa*, inert. Anything that I observe is *jaḍa*, inert. I am a conscious being, the only significant thing in this entire universe of words and meanings, names and forms.

See the meaning of that. Free of fear, I am. Free of afflictions, I am. Free of guilt or hurt, I am comfortable being myself. If this is true, you can tell yourself "it is easy to be myself". Being myself is effortless, natural to me. *Oṃ śāntiḥ śāntiḥ śāntiḥ.*

To access the live session, click **HERE** or scan the QR code given below:

I AM *ASAṄGA*, THE CHANGELESS AWARENESS

viśvaṃ darpaṇadṛśyamānanagarītulyaṃ nijāntargataṃ
paśyannātmani māyayā bahirivodbhūtaṃ yathā nidrayā |
yaḥ sākṣātkurute prabodhasamaye svātmānamevādvayaṃ
tasmai śrīgurumūrtaye nama idaṃ śrīdakṣiṇāmūrtaye ||

I take the time to arrive. Assuming the posture, I ensure that the head, neck, and back are in a single line. My eyes are softly closed. I connect with the breathing, visualizing with every inhalation how I am rejuvenating this body with fresh oxygen, and with every exhalation, I visualize the toxins and the *tamas* leaving the body. I take long, full, deep, conscious breaths. The mind is fully occupied in watching the full, deep breathing. If the mind strays, I gently bring it back. As I am sitting here enjoying my breathing, I remind myself there is nothing to do right now, nowhere to go, nothing to achieve, nothing to gain, nothing to lose. This is the truth of the self, and repeating the truth of the self as affirmations can be very relaxing. I bring the attention back to the breathing, if it has strayed. I focus on the sensation of the cool in-breath entering the nostrils and the slightly warm air leaving. There is nothing to do but breathe. There is nothing to do other than to just be.

Bringing the awareness to the body, I observe the body. Who is this observer? Who is the one watching the body? Awareness, consciousness with a name: *sākṣin*. What is this body? Is it outside awareness, outside consciousness? *Idam śarīram,* this body, I can watch. It is consciousness with another name, form, status; consciousness as object, body, consciousness as objectifier, I, *aham*. When I watch this body, I see that there are many things beyond my control. There are many things I cannot change: my height, my weight, the color of my skin, and my predilection to certain ailments. This is how the body is. As I identify with the observer, I can see that I am not just this body. I am *saccidānanda,* without boundaries.

There are no limits. The body occupies a certain space, a certain time. It has an origin, is subject to aging, disease, destruction. I, the watcher, my nature is free. No birth, no death, no disease. This body is my body, I can say. But, I am without boundaries. I am life, without boundaries. Sentience, without limits. I let this sink in.

Now, I watch the mind. Without shunning the thoughts or clinging to the thoughts or running after the thoughts, I just watch the mind. Thoughts come, thoughts go. By the time I even register the fact that a thought is born, it is gone. Born is gone. Thought born, thought is, thought gone. Gone, born, is. Born, gone. I am a steady windless flame of consciousness that watches the birth and departure of the thoughts on this vast limitless canvas. Thoughts come and go like a movie being projected on a screen. I am free from the drama of the thoughts and the emotions, which are also thoughts. Whatever is happening on the movie does not affect the screen. I am Free of this mind, free of its acrobatics. Up and down it goes, all around it goes. I am the stillness, like a placid lake, free of ripples, waves.

Now I move to observe the senses. I begin with the sense of touch. Legs touch one another. The hips touch the seat. I just observe. Clothes touch the body. The tongue touches the teeth. To highlight the sense of touch, I half open the eyes and slowly, softly close them. Can I sense the touch of the top eyelid on the bottom eyelid? One more time, I open the eyes partially and softly close.

Asaṅgo'ham, I am uninvolved in the activities of the body, mind, senses. I am *asaṃga*. Free. Whole. Present. There is no guilt, no hurt. Those are the just thoughts that rise and fall in the mind. Likewise, sorrow, anger, and any form of emotional pain are just extended thoughts, clinging on to one another, still rising and falling in the mind. I am the unmoving, all pervasive consciousness. Awareness without size, with no date of birth, no destruction, and no change. That which is aware of changes has got to be changeless.

This is *nirvikāraḥ,* changeless consciousness. I, *aham,* am free, whole, all pervasive, without a second, and joyous by nature. This is my story. This is my reality. It is easy to be just be. It is easy to be free. It is easy to be me. *Oṃ śāntiḥ śāntiḥ śāntiḥ.*

To access the live session, click HERE or scan the QR code given above.

BEING STILL

The posture is important for meditation. The head, neck, and back are in a single line. The shoulders are not hunched over. As much as possible, this posture is held steadily and the head is not allowed to droop forward because that often leads to sleep. The breathing is even, soft, and gentle.

Mornings are good time for contemplation because one is fresh, rested and ready to go throughout the day. Once one gets going, it is difficult to find the time to be with oneself. There are endless items on the agenda, and each one seems to scream with an urgency that defies understanding. In this scenario, it is easy to forget oneself. The sense organs and mind are overactive and are preoccupied with various pursuits. Insufficient inward focus leads to an unbalanced state that is reflected in the contemporary society, all too often recognized in oneself.

One is so addicted to doing that being still seems to be the aberration, a strange anomaly to the collective practices that are prevalent. Yet it is in those moments of stillness and being with oneself that great strides are made in all fields. It is in those moments of stillness that one finds the center, the inspiration, the core of one's being. The inspiration is nothing but *Īśvara*. Lord Krishna says in the Bhagavad Gita that any glory present in any being is his alone.

Achieving the stillness is not difficult. Once one is disengaged from the addiction to activity by making time to contemplate, one is already still. Being still is being the observer. I observe the body part by part, starting with the head, neck and shoulders. There is a lot of activity in the head to keep the body still. The activity goes without my participation. In fact, the observer, the being that is still, is uninvolved in the activity. The witness is uninvolved, for example, in all the signals sent by the brain to keep the vertebrae stacked upon each other to maintain the posture.

The facial muscles are relaxed as I observe the face, yet there is activity. The skin is constantly cleaning– that is its job: self-cleaning itself through the pores. The sense of touch is active. The muscles that hold up the face are relaxed, but there is activity. I, the observer, am still, uninvolved. As the inward gaze softly falls on the front of the body, again there is activity. I notice the activity. The chest rises and falls with the breathing. As the lungs expand, The stomach and the abdomen also join in the rising and falling. The one who notices all this is still, and does not go up and down with the breath. The digestive organs are active. The endocrine glands active. The observer just being; there is no doing , just being. Even the act of observing is not an action, it is just being. The back of the body likewise is active. The watcher of the back of the body is still.

Out of this stillness arises movement, like the stillness of the night yielding to the day. The upper back, the mid back, and the lower back are all active and engaged; I am the observer, *sākṣin*, still, still, still. The right side of the body is active; I am still. The arm, The right elbow, the forearm, the right hand with all its fingers are relaxed, with some activity going on. I am still. I observe the left side of the body: the left arm, elbow, forearm, hand, and left fingers. Despite anything happening on the left side of the body, I am *asaṅga:* still, uninvolved. Observing is not doing. It is an observation that takes place without effort. Being disengaged from action is a natural state. It is the *svarūpa* of the *ātman*, the nature of the "I."

The self is *aluptadṛk*, the eternal observer. What about the legs? Now I am observing the right hip, right thigh, the knee, the muscles below the knee, ankle, and the right foot. I do the same on the left side; I observe the whole leg, part by part. Now I observe the body as though I am sitting in front of a full length mirror. I can also observe what is happening inside. I can feel the blood rushing to the various extremities, I can sense the dull thud of the heart beating. All movement is born of stillness, sustained by stillness, and resolves into that stillness.

Now, I watch the breathing without altering the breath. I observe the movement. Each breath revitalizes the body, bathes the cells in oxygen, aerates the blood, and removes toxins. How does this activity take place? Despite my non-action, the body is sustained, detoxified, energized, and kept alive. *Prāṇo vai Īśvaraḥ*– the *prāṇa* that moves all over the body, the life force– is born of stillness. The observer, the "I", precedes the *prāṇa*.

Now I observe the mind. There is so much activity, so many thoughts, so many plans, and so many emotions. Still, the watcher of the mind is *asaṅga,* uninvolved. I let the effortless gaze of the seer fall on the mind, like the rays of the rising sun falling upon the earth and lighting up everything. Thoughts come and go, emotions come, they go, and I am still. Being still is being free. Knowing stillness is knowing freedom. Observing the mind without any effort, I allow the chant to arise from the depth of the mind without any effort. Just as the sun ray kisses the earth, a seedling sprouts. The light of the Atma blesses the mind, the chant sprouts: soft and vulnerable, yet strong, with a will to survive.

The chant "*Oṃ Īśāya namaḥ*" is placed in the mind effortlessly, repeatedly. The chant is repeatedly watered by the awareness; the chant is alive. Like a nascent sprout, it gains strength; it grows without effort. There is no doing, just being. When I chant, it is effortless; when I drop the chant, it is still effortless. Stillness continues. The mind sinks into the heart. What prevails is stillness. There is no will at all.

When I just am, the will is suspended. No will is required to hear these words, because hearing just takes place. If the ears are functioning and there are words to hear, hearing takes place. Hearing is an action that arises from stillness. Sound arises from stillness, and resolves into stillness, rising from the stillness– *Hare Krishna, Hare Krishna, Hare Krishna, Krishna, Krishna, Hare Hare*– and drops into the stillness.
Sound, stillness, sound. Stillness, sound, stillness. Chant, consciousness, chant.
Consciousness, chant consciousness. Chant consciousness, chant.

Can sound disturb stillness? Can the chant disturb consciousness? Sound rises from stillness, which is the truth of sound. Stillness is the content of sound. Stillness is not opposed to sound; sound is *mithyā*. It emerges from, and resolves into, stillness. Ultimately there is no thing called stillness– it is a relational word. When sound ultimately does not exist, how can there be something called stillness? The nameless, formless, attribute-free presence which exists is stillness. That stillness is I, the source of everything, the source of creation, *Brahman*. Being still is being free. Knowing stillness is knowing freedom. The chant is again invited to abide in the mind repeatedly, gently. The chant resolves into the stillness, the silence. There is no will. There is no hurry. Being is being still. Being is knowing. Stillness is limitlessness. Being still is being free. Being free is being who I am. If you are comfortable being still, being free, acknowledge that to yourself: "I am comfortable being myself." Om *śāntiḥ, śāntiḥ, śāntiḥ.*

To access the live session, click **HERE** or scan the QR code given below:

RELATING TO THE ORDER

Oṃ viśvaṃ darpaṇadṛśyamānanagarītulyaṃ nijāntargataṃ
paśyannātmani māyayā bahirivodbhūtaṃ yathā nidrayā
yaḥ sākṣātkurute prabodhasamaye svātmānamevādvayaṃ
tasmai śrīgurumūrtaye nama idaṃ śrīdakṣiṇāmūrtaye

I, the meditator, a self-conscious being, am an individual with my own life, and my thoughts, my likes, and my dislikes all connected to the total. A conscious being connecting to consciousness is like a tree relating to the forest. The tree is already related to the forest, just as I, the individual conscious being, I am already related to *Īśvara*, the total. In meditation, this connection is simply highlighted through a chant.

I take the time to assume the posture conducive to focus. Firming up the posture, hands clasped on the lap, thumbs touching, I begin watching the breathing and offloading all things that are supposed to be outside, but has gained entry without my knowledge, like stowaways. I take the time to offload the world, the inner internalized world on my own. How is this done? I visualize the people, one by one, who have crept under the skin. I grant them the freedom to be whoever and however they are. In so doing, I find myself free of the unfulfilled hopes and desires that they will change, and from the resentful thoughts that they should have been different. In the instances and areas where I am unable to grant this freedom, I simply ask for help from the very source, responsible for this internalization, which is *Bhagavān* in the form of psychological order. *tasmai namaḥ, tasmai namaḥ. Hey Bhagavan*, I acknowledge that I have no power over this internalization. Some things in the form of internalized feelings are like calluses which will not go easily.

I did not ask to be born. I did not ask for the family of birth, for this background, for this parentage. Sometimes, I am at a loss about how to relate without losing my composure or my sanity.

The effects of the background run deep and could cause an impediment in my pursuit of this teaching. H*are Rama hare Rama, Rama, Rama, hare, hare*.

The word "hari" or "hara" means the one who takes away that which does not belong. When I can see that I am powerless in certain areas, I need to plug into the source of power, *Īśvara*. I know I am overpowered sometimes by thoughts, and sometimes too by emotions, fears, notions, beliefs, which are inimical to my spiritual evolution. I must let go of these in order to grow. Hey *Bhagavan*, Help me to externalize that which does not belong within. I have no power over my anger; I cannot even see it coming. It is the same with grief, and the same with fear. My psychological background is in keeping with my *karmic* background. My parentage, *karmic* background, given by you. My psychological profile, given by you. Nay, it is in fact you in the form of my *karma*. It is you in the form of my reactions. It is all you. I hand over my psychological profile to you.

Hey Govinda! Hey Gopāla!

When I hand over to you the *karma* that has brought forth this body-mind-sense complex, it is no longer my *karma*. When I hand over to You my feelings, thoughts, helplessness, and fears, they are no longer mine. They are part of the psychological order that is you. I am s*accidānanda*– free, present, unassailed by afflictions and strong in the face of difficulties and challenges. Difficulties are You. Challenges, too, are some of your many faces, in the facets of my life. Teach me O *Bhagavan* to see this. Can I see Your presence in every challenge I have had to face in the past? Can I see your face in the challenges that confront me right now?

Sthāne, it is in order. Given this background, that a person would have these kinds of feelings is in order. Challenges are also in order. That which I considered in disorder, is also in order: one non-dual, mega, vast order. Order means it is predictable. It is Law. Not a law given by *Īśvara*, but Law in the form of that very *Īśvara*. It Law non-separate from *Bhagavān*. Can I rest, relax in this order, knowing that there is not much to do, other than to just be? Can I let go a bit more and still a bit more, especially when I feel that I have reached the threshold of letting go? I let go of the threshold itself. Can I see this *jagat* as a city reflected in a big mirror? Animals, plants, flora and fauna walk by this mirror, as do the days and weather patterns: rain, clouds, sun, night, day, sunrise, sunset... all is witnessed through this big mirror reflecting the *jagat*. I am the watcher, not the reflection. I am not one of the objects that can be reflected. As a watcher, I can enjoy this marvelous show of light, sound, sun, moon, wind, and water. The five elements dance like *Naṭarāja*. I am the stillness watching the dance, unaffected by the movements while marveling at the flawless choreography of the dance. All is reflected in the mirror. The *jagat* is like a city that goes by in the mirror. People go, people come. Moving things are reflecting in the mirror, and stationary things are also reflected in the same mirror... buildings, houses, mountains, lakes, and more.

This *jagat* is akin to city reflected in a mirror. When rain comes, it is the city that is drenched, not the mirror. When fog comes, it is the city that is enveloped in the fog, not the mirror. If I can appreciate this, I can also see that when I look deeper, even my *antaḥkaraṇa* is reflected in the mirror, as it were. My thoughts, my sad thoughts of self-pity and victimization do not affect the mirror. Angry thoughts, and thoughts of destruction do not destroy the mirror. Fearful thoughts do not make the mirror run away. Helpless thoughts do not victimize the mirror. My inner *jagat*– thoughts, notions, regrets, guilt, hurt, pains, sorrows, and few joys– all of it is seen through the mirror.

Can I take a step further and see I am this mirror, clear and free of all the things that I reflect, that I observe, *saccidānanda*? Unto that, *namaḥ*. *Tasmai namaḥ*, *tasmai namaḥ*.

Unto that all-knowledge that lights up this *buddhi* to see the truth of who I am, *tasmai namaḥ*, *tasmai namaḥ*, *tasmai namaḥ*. *Oṃ śāntiḥ śāntiḥ śāntiḥ*.

To access the live session, click **HERE** or scan the QR code given below:

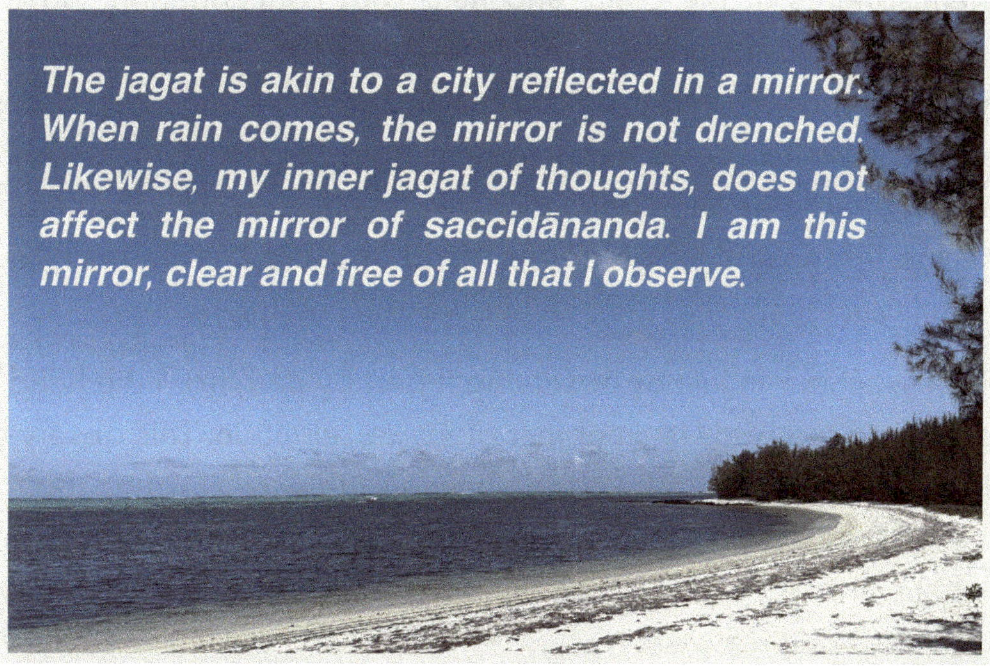

The jagat is akin to a city reflected in a mirror. When rain comes, the mirror is not drenched. Likewise, my inner jagat of thoughts, does not affect the mirror of saccidānanda. I am this mirror, clear and free of all that I observe.

JYOTIṢĀM JYOTIḤ: THE LIGHT OF ALL LIGHTS

Taking the time to arrive, connect with your presence. Tell yourself, "I am here now." Begin with a few rounds of *nāḍī śuddhi*, alternate nostril breathing. To do that, shut off the right nostril with the thumb, breathe in through the left, shut off the left nostril with the fingers, breathe out through the right. Breathe in again through the left, and breathe out through the right. Continue at your own pace in this manner, making sure that you breathe in through the same nostril out of which you have just exhaled.

As this practice is underway, I make sure that the posture is erect with the head, neck and back in a single straight line. The face is soft. The shoulders are not rising up to the ears. With each breath, I visualize myself surrendering to the breathing. No tension, no holding, just breathing. Six minutes of this practice is said to totally calm the mind, balance the hemispheres of the brain, and help with concentration. Now, we can try doubling the time of exhalation by simply counting the inhalation to four and the exhalation eight. Long, deep, and if possible, silent *prāṇāyāma*. There is nothing to do right now except just to be a conscious simple being. *Oṃ bhūrbhuvaḥ svaḥ tatsaviturvareṇyaṃ bhargo devasya dhīmahi dhiyo yo naḥ pracodayāt.* The next time you inhale through the left nostril, let go off the hand and breathe normally. If there is an increased tranquility, it means that the practice was successful.

Scanning the body, I check in just by observing it part by part, from the head to the toes. I am the observer and the body is an object of my observation. This observation can be self-guided. I go from observing the head, face, all the way down to the toes, part by part, silently. Then I visualize myself seated in front of a full length mirror, just watching this body do whatever it does. This is how the body is, an object of my observation.

The object is not the subject. A*ham* is "I" and the body is *idam*, an object of "this" cognition. *Aham* is not *idam. Idam* comes, *idam* goes. Anything that I refer to with the word *idam* comes and goes, but *aham* always here, now. *Idam is* finite. *Aham is* eternal, infinite. *Idam* is insentient, but *aham* is sentient. Now I simply watch the mind, without chasing after the thoughts or running away from them. If I start to identify with the thoughts, I gently extricate myself, and return to the place of the observer.

When I say that mind is *idam, it is aham* observing the *idam. Idam* is insentient; *aham* is sentient. *Idam* is many and varied; *aham is the* only thing there is, non-dually one. *Idam* is object. *Aham* is the subject. *Idam* is *anātman*, *aham* is *ātman. Idam* is changing. *Aham* is *nirvikāraḥ*, unchanging, and free of all modifications. *Idam* is the object of cognition. *Aham* is the cognizer, nay it is the very consciousness, in whose presence *jñātṛ* and *jñeya* –the knower and the known– come to light.

Hey Govinda! Hey Gopāla!

Hearing happens, hearing takes place. When there is a sound, it is heard. *Aham* is the hearer: the now hearer, now thinker, now seer, and now observer. Who am I really? The hearer comes, the hearer resolves. *Hare Rama, hare Rama, Rama, Rama, hare, hare*. The "I" is now a hearer, now an observer. When the sound resolves after the chant, who am I? The hearer is gone. When there is nothing to observe, who am I? The Seer, the observer, the hearer, and the knower, are all resolved; all are gone. When thoughts are absent, like in sleep, who am I? I am longer a thinker. I simply am.

All there is a presence that I can scarcely call mine. It is an all pervasive presence, unchanging, recognized as the known. It is *is-ness*, recognized as I, it is *am-ness*. It is *śuddha-caitanya*, consciousness unconditioned by name or form. It is forever the same– the unchanging, inexhaustible, all pervading presence.

It is all pervading because it pervades the observer and the objects of observation. Everything is included in this presence– the body is not outside this conscious presence; the mind is not outside this conscious presence. The senses also are within this conscious presence. All objects are naught but name and form, included in consciousness. The observer is also included in consciousness.

Who am I? I am free, whole. I am neither the observer, nor the observed. I am that which includes both and transcends them also. I am *jyotiṣām jyotiḥ,* the light of all lights, in whose presence everything lights up, becomes evident. The light that is uninvolved in the drama, lights up the drama, but is not part of it. I am that consciousness in whose presence everything comes to light; I am the revealer. I reclaim this identity. I am consciousness, free of name and form. I am whole, ever present, limitless. This presence – sacred, free and infinite –I choose to inhabit, at least for today. *Oṃ śānti̱ḥ śānti̱ḥ śānti̱ḥ*.

To access the live session, click **HERE** or scan the QR code given below:

THE TRUTH OF ONESELF

The seat is stable and comfortable; not so comfortable that sleep will come, but not so uncomfortable that one has to keep shifting, moving. The *Bhagavad-Gita* leads us through the practice of meditation, teaching us specific things that one can do to prepare oneself. The head, neck and back are held comfortably in a single straight line. The eyes are not restless. Two more instructions are given in the *Bhagavad-Gita*. One must breathe consciously so that the inhalation and the exhalation are more or less of the same length. It is important to keep the external world outside, not letting it be a baggage in the *buddhi*.

We visualize the mother. This is how she is, she was, in my perception. Retaining the love and caring for the mother, I grant her the freedom to be whoever she was, however she is. In so doing, I find myself freed of the expectation that she should have been different or that she should be different. I visualize the father. This is how he was, this is how he is, in my perception. Retaining the care and love for the father, I grant him the freedom to be whoever he was, however he is. This means that many of my expectations may not have been fulfilled, may not ever be fulfilled either. Acknowledging that frees me from those very expectations. Towards anybody currently in one's life, it is possible to do the same thing. Visualize the person. Grant them the freedom to be however they are, *in your perception*. This is how they are. If residual feelings that one cannot handle persist, one can offer them to *Bhagavān*.

Hey Bhagavan, grant me the courage to change the things that I can and the acceptance to deal with the things that I cannot change. Grant me the wisdom to know the difference between what I cannot change and what can be changed.

Then, I come back to watching this body, which is external to me, yet internalized in the form of various notions. This is how the body is. There are many things I cannot change. *Oṃ namaḥ, Oṃ namaḥ, Oṃ namaḥ. Oṃ.* Word for body in Sanskrit is *deha–dahana yogyatvāt,* that which is fit to be consigned to the flames at the end of life. *Śarīram, śīryamāṇa svabhāvāt*, is another word is *śarīram,* which means that which is fit for disintegration at the end of life. Such words help us to be objective with regard to the body. This body is a house for me, *dehin,* the one indweller unaffected by what happens with the body: the observer, *sākṣīn.*

I move to watch the mind. Dispassionately, I let the thoughts come and I let them go. I am the canvas on which various mental scenarios get played. Free, I am in the form of the observer. I am all-knowledge. Unruffled I am. The motion of the mind does not affect the "I." I watch the mind ,knowing that when it is watched, the mind naturally is tranquil. The practice of *japa* strengthens the mind to stay in the tranquil state. I give the mind a job to chant - *Oṃ namaḥ śivāya. Śivāya*, unto that most auspicious one which is the Truth of myself, free of all blemishes: *namaḥ*, my salutations. *Oṃ* is a sound of blessing.

I place the mantra in the mind and get ready for the chanting, remembering always to bring the mind back repeatedly, whenever it goes away. I do this gently, repeatedly. The second thing to remember is that distractions happen between in the space between two chants. If I pay close attention to the space between the chants, it lessens the distractions. I start chanting mentally now.

Allow the chant to stop. Closely watch the spaces between the chants, as I chant and again pick up the chant silently, as soon as I stop. *Oṃ namaḥ śivāya Oṃ Oṃ Oṃ.* Let the chant drop. Again, I watch the spaces between the chants and pick it up as soon as the chant stops. *Oṃ namaḥ śivāya Oṃ Oṃ Oṃ.*

Let the chant drop. *Eko devaḥ,* one self-effulgent consciousness. *Sarvabhūteṣu gūḍhāḥ,* hidden in all beings. *Sarvavyāpī,* all pervasive. *Sarvabhūtāntarātmā,* the truth of everything. *Karmādhyakṣa,* the one that gives the results of action. *Sākṣī, cetā,* the one in whose presence everything comes to light. *Kevalo nirguṇaśca,* the only thing that is, free of attributes, free of name, free of form. This is my Reality. May I accept it! May I see it! May I be it! *Oṃ śāntiḥ śāntiḥ śāntiḥ.*

To access the live session, click **HERE** or scan the QR code given below:

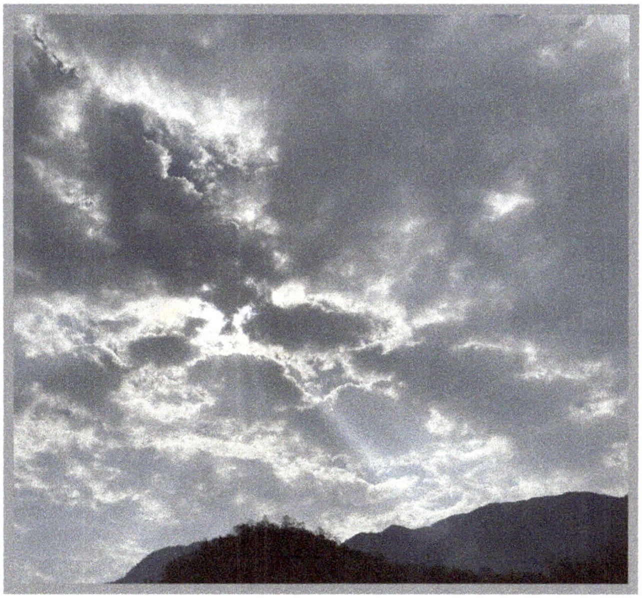

THE TRAVELER AND THE DESTINATION ARE ONE

Oṃ prātaḥ smarāmi hṛdi saṁsphuradātmatattvaṁ; saccitsukhaṁ paramahaṁsagatiṁ turīyam; yatsvapnajāgarasuṣuptimavaiti nityaṁ; tadbrahma niṣkalamahaṁ na ca bhūtasaṅghaḥ.

These morning musings by *Ādi Śaṃkara* give us a glimpse of how to connect with oneself. In preparation for this *upadeśa*, teaching, I take the time to arrive and find my center. *The center is always calm, even in the eye of a storm. It is śāntam, sukham, niścalam - unmoving, niṣkalam - partless.* I ensure that I have assumed the most conducive posture for this meditation, which effortlessly helps me find the center.

I connect with the breathing. With each in-breath, I visualize inhabiting the body more fully, becoming more present. With every exhalation, I let go of distraction, resistance, and obstacles–*pratibandha*. I take long, deep, and (if possible) silent breaths. With each in-breath, I can say to myself, "this body is my body", alright. But I am life without boundaries. This mind is mine, true. But I transcend the mind. I am without boundaries. One can say that the *prāṇa* which keeps the body alive is my *prāṇa*, but I am that life force which powers even the *prāṇa* to bless this body. With each breath, I can will myself to go to a quieter place, a tranquil place where there is no conflict. It is a place of harmony that is very familiar which I long to inhabit. The time to inhabit it is now.

When I watch the mind, I can see the thoughts coming in and out, like people getting in and out of a crowded train. I am not the participant. I have nowhere to go, nothing to gain, nothing to lose. I am the sojourner, whose destiny and journey are one in the same.

Prātaḥ smarāmi, in the mornings, I muse and recall *ātmatattva*, the truth of myself that is ever present like even the heartbeat. Just as the heartbeat is regular, never absent, predictable, and reassuring, so too is my presence.

I, *aham*, *aham*. Obtaining as I, who is right now? The observer. Even when I do not observe, I still am. I am still, still I am.

prātaḥ smarāmi hṛdi saṁsphuradātmatattvaṁ What is the nature of this I? *Saccitsukhaṁ*, the source of all existence. *Sat*, I am *Sat:* self-standing, independent, self-evident, self-luminous existence. Free and untethered, I am, *aham*. I am *Cit*– sentience, consciousness, awareness. I am awareness personified even when there is nothing to be aware of, nothing to be conscious of. All that is here, non-separate from I, consciousness. My presence does not come to an end. Eternal, *nitya*, *ānandasvarūpa*, *sukhasvarūpa*. It is reassuring, it is forever. Forever is reassuring, because I long for it. I long for whatever I already am, *saccitsukhaṁ*, *ātmatattvam*.

Where is this *ātmatattva*? It is right where I recognize I, myself, *aham*. It is the goal of all *mahātmas*, *paramahaṁsagati*, it is. *Aham*, the truth of this I is the goal of the most exalted sages, who with the power of their knowledge abide in this effortlessly, all the time. I walk in their footsteps, grateful for a little glimpse in and through my crowded days, crowded ways of being. I am blessed by the vision of no division, thanks to the weight of this lineage of exalted ones. How do I recognize this *ātmatattvam* as that which is the Truth of the waking, dreaming and sleeping states? *Yat ātmatattvam svapnajāgarasuṣuptimavaiti nityaṁ.*

I know, I am. I know. Always I know that I am the unaffected inhabiter of the waking, dream and deep sleep states; I am *turīyā*, ever awakened. Never absent, I am *aluptadṛk*, the constant seer, who is never missing; I am the one who meanders effortlessly, visiting the various states – sleep, dream, and waking. I am that *Brahman*, partless, *niṣkalam*.

The body has parts. The mind has various states. Emotions come and go. *Ahaṃkāra,* the ego, rises and falls. I am the unchanging *ātman*, free, whole.

I am *Brahman, ātma*, *Brahman* – one and the same, synonyms. I am the indweller of this body-mind-sense complex. This is a well ventilated room, like a hotel room. I am a visitor of this *jagat*. I come with a mobile hotel room. It takes me wherever I want to go. Just as I am not affected by the hotel room, in the same way, I am not affected by this body-mind-sense complex.

Bhūtasaṅghaḥ na aham, I am not the sack of flesh, blood, bones. I am that which blesses this body-mind complex with sentience, existence. Like a puppeteer, bringing the show to life, I hold the string of this body-mind complex. *Brahman aham, ātmatattvaḥ aham, niṣkalam,* partless *aham*, *turīyaḥ aham*, *saccitsukhaḥ aham*. This is my truth. This is my reality. Let me own this up. Let me see this. Let me be this, at least for today. *Oṃ śānti̱ḥ śānti̱ḥ śānti̱ḥ.*

To access the live session, click **HERE** or scan the QR code given below:

THE GIVER AND THE GIVEN

This body was given. I did not make it. I do not even know the names of all the organs, processes, bones, muscles that make up the anatomy of this body. It is given to me, a gift because of which I can move. I can go about my day, my life. The ability to observe the body is also given. Effortless it is to observe this body, and as I turn the inward gaze to watch the body, I find that it comes naturally to me without any exertion.

As I observe the body, it is clear that the body is not myself. There are many dissimilarities right at the start that one can see. The body is *jaḍa,* inert, whereas I am sentient. This was given. This is how it is. The body is always changing, through childhood, youth, and old age, and also day by day: now it is healthy, now it is sick, now it feels cold, now it feels hot.

In contrast, I am changeless. How do I know I am changeless? Because I can observe the changes. If I were subject to changes, I would not be able to observe the changes taking place in the body. The body is an object and can be objectified. In contrast, I am the subject. The body is put together. See the truth of this, put together. This is very clear when we watch the growth of the baby in the mother's womb - part by part, it grows. I am partless. The body has a birth date, where friends gather and wish it happy birthday. The body also has the date of expiration, an expiry date. There again, loved ones gather and mourn the departure of the body. I am the birth-less, deathless, awareness-consciousness. The body needs maintenance, it is falling apart at regular intervals. I am maintenance free. Why? Because there are no parts. There is no sickness, no beginning, no end. The body is a host of diseases. I am disease free. The body is put together for me, consciousness, to as-though abide in. The body is therefore *samhata*, put together, for my sake. Consider the meaning of this. I am *asamhata:* not put together. I can say "I am the indweller of this body" if I am clear about the meaning of this statement: I am the indweller of this body, much like space is the indweller of this room and gets a new name, "room space." I, consciousness, awareness, who am free, clear, and of the nature of light, dwell this body like space dwells a room. If the room falls apart, it does not affect space. The afflictions of the body do not affect me. The body given but what about consciousness? Consciousness simply is, it is the meaning of the word "I".

The mind is also given. Like the body, it is different from I. The mind is the object of observation. In truth, I am sentient, alive without any prop, alive without needing to breathe. The mind is shining in borrowed light of awareness: the mind is inert, the mind is changing. I am changeless. The mind is restless, whereas I am peaceful, tranquil, and free of movement. The mind is full of doubts. I free of doubt. The mind ages. I am ageless. The mind is a storehouse of memories. I am free, all-knowledge, and the observer of the memories. The mind is *duḥkhālaya,* an abode of sorrow. I am free, *ānanda:* not even a shadow of sorrow can touch me. The mind is jumpy, subject to fear. Consciousness is *abhaya*: no fear, it is I. Guilt, hurt, regret, anger, and pain, are properties of the mind. I am the canvas over which these emotions unfold.

I am the space-like consciousness, unaffected when clouds of depression rain, *duḥkha*. The mind is given. The body is given. The senses are given. The organs of action are given. Is there a giver? Who is this giver? Did the cells randomly assemble themselves to form the kidneys, lungs, and brain? Nothing random is in this *jagat,* starting with my own body. I find that it is very orderly and predictable. Various body parts, the mind, and the senses all follow laws. We can study the behavior of the kidneys. That is why we can say when the kidneys are well. What are the possible diseases these organs can get? Predictable. How to overcome the diseases is also given in the form of the *buddhi*, the intellect, to do research into the diseases. It is given.

Who is the giver? Who is this giver in whose presence everything comes to life? Who is this vast storehouse of knowledge that can create and project this flawless universe, which includes my own body, my own mind, my own senses, my own background, my own parentage, my fears, my tears and my ability to transcend all of those to pursue this knowledge. If my own fears are included in the *jagat,* I can no longer call them mine. They are an expression of the *karmic* order and the psychological order. In the presence of a certain threat, that a *jīva* will respond with fear is a given. The ability to overcome the fear also given. Free will is given. The ability to abuse the free will is also given. All that which is given is non-separate from the giver, like even my dream. All the beings in my dream are non-separate from me: they come from my memories, my desires. They are given, non-separate from the giver. In everything that is given, the presence of the giver shines. I am that shine. *Saccidānanda, Brahman, brahmātmān*, non-separate from the giver. See that, be that. *Oṃ śāntiḥ śāntiḥ śāntiḥ*.

To access the live session, click **HERE** or scan the QR code given below:

EVER CONNECTED, NEVER ALIENATED

This universe is not outside myself, an individual endowed with the body, with the mind, senses, likes, dislikes. In fact, all these comprise the *jagat* for this conscious being, I. The *jagat* starts with my body. The changing body, the changeless I, are as though in one place. They have to be because the changing depends on the changeless. Through this body-mind complex, I am connected to the vast, intelligent universe: a universe filled with wonders, where everything is predictable, unfolding according to laws.

Starting with my breathing, I take the time to watch the breath and see that the rhythmic inhalations and exhalations correspond to the rhythms of the *jagat* like the waves touching the shore and going back. They too are in the rhythm. There is an order. My breathing itself is a wonder. When I look at it, I see nothing but *Bhagavān, Īśvara*. How do the lungs open to receive *vāyu, this Brahman. namaste vāyu tvameva pratyakṣaṃ brahmāsi.*

Namaste to *vāyu*, air. You are not just one of the five elements, You are the palpable *Brahman,* which cannot be objectified. How do the lungs open to receive the air? What are the mechanisms by which the impurities are filtered? How do these impurities get cast out again through the exhalation? It is due to *Īśvara* in the form of the respiratory order. When I look at it this way, it is no longer my breathing, my *prāṇa.* It is a law. I am one with everything that breaths. Everything that depends upon oxygen to be alive, I am one with all that breathes: dogs, cats, cows, birds, and even reptiles. Any disturbances in the order is also part of the order. The mega order is big enough to have disturbances, to include anything that doesn't work. *namaste astu bhagavan.* I see the same knowledge of *Īśvara* abiding in this body as I do *deha vīkṣaṇa.*

I watch the body. It is a marvel, a miracle. Everything is how it should be. *Sthāne,* all is well. Digestion takes place. Circulation takes place. It is a law. Any disturbances in the body also part of the law, perhaps another law, *kārmic* order. My senses– sight, hearing, touch, taste, and smell–all function how they need to without my doing anything. It is an order. Wherever there are eyes they see, the eyes of a cow, cat, dog. *namaste astu bhagavan*

Unto that form of *Bhagavān* which blesses the eyes to see, the ears to hear, *namaḥ*. *namaḥ* to that consciousness that operates my senses. The anatomical order is marvel, a miracle. It is the same everywhere without exception. That is why there can be branches of knowledge; anatomy, physiology, and other -ologies are words that convey *Bhagavān*. *namaste astu. hey Bhagavan.*

In this way I am connected to *Bhagavān,* never alone, never alienated. All I have to do is breathe to sense this connection. Another order is the psychological order. There too is a method. That given this background, one would have certain issues, is not surprising. It's a law. Whenever a desire is thwarted, anger comes. It's a law. See that. When I can appreciate this, it is no longer my anger. It is in order, an orderly response, a reaction to a given situation of non-wish fulfillment. Anger is a given, it is part of the order. The free will to manage this anger so that I do not target myself or others is also given, is also part of the order.

Sorrow is given. There is always a reason; that too is given. It is a response to loss, real or perceived. Sadness is in order. The methods to address the sadness also in order. No longer is it my sadness, my anger, my fear. If it is a law, an orderly response or a reaction to certain situations, I can let it go. I need not claim it as mine. I can be objective.

First, I can be appreciative of this order. I can look upon the anger dispassionately, as I would a volcano. The burning lava is there to see. Yes, it may be dormant now, but it has everything in it to erupt. I can be dispassionate, objective towards my anger in the light of this vision. If anger is justified, so too are the methods to manage it. The order is incomplete without the free will to manage the emotions. I can also appreciate the *kārmic* order, which governs everything, starting with my birth, my parentage, my body, my mind, and my senses. *namaste astu bhagavan*

Whatever joys I experience are in order. My challenges are also in order. If I look around, I see the same order in everybody's life. They do have joys, they do have challenges. Therefore, I need not own up these challenges as mine. They are things that needs to be addressed through prayer, emotional growth, and acceptance. *Namaste astu bhagavan.*

Eko devaḥ, one effulgent consciousness. *sarvabhūteṣu gūḍhāḥ,* abiding, hidden in all beings.*sarvavyāpī,* all pervasive. *Sarvabhūtāntarātmā,* one that is the truth of all creation. *karmādhyakṣa,* the one in charge of the law of karma. S*arvabhūtādivāsā*, that which abides all beings. *Sākṣī,* which obtains in me as the witness. *Cetā,* in whose presence everything functions. K*evalaḥ,* non-dually one. *Nirguṇaśca,* whose form is really no form. This I have to see. This I have to be. *Oṃ śāntiḥ śāntiḥ śāntiḥ.*

To access the live session, click **HERE** or scan the QR code given below:

CONSCIOUSNESS IS NOT AN OBJECT

Oṃ hrīṃ dakṣiṇāmūrtaye tubhyaṃ vaṭamūlanivasine
dhyānaikaniratāṅgāya namo rūdraya śambhave hrīṃ Oṃ

Hearing takes place. When the mind is behind the ears, hearing happens without the operation of the will. *Hare Rama*–hearing happens. *Hare Rama, Rama Rama hare hare*

What is allowing the hearing to happen? Consciousness, "I," *aham*. When I chant *Oṃ namaḥ śivāya,* the chant is. Chant-consciousness is. When there is no chant, no-chant-consciousness, no-chant-awareness is. This awareness is "I." Consciousness is not an object.

If we do an exercise listing various objects, we will find consciousness is not an object. Visualize the objects being listed now:
Apple, house, river, sun, tree, consciousness.
Temple, book, orange, umbrella, consciousness.
Table, chair, carpet, consciousness.
Paper, mountain, rose flower, desk, consciousness.
Rope, snake, pot, clay, consciousness.
Earth, water, fire, air, space, time, consciousness.

What happens when the word consciousness is heard? No object arises. The mind draws a blank. All objects shine in my awareness. Awareness itself is free of objects. An object *is*. Consciousness *is*. Without an object, consciousness still *is*. Train the mind to associate the word consciousness with I, *aham*.

Place the chant *Oṃ namaḥ śivāya* in the mind and chant mentally. The chant must not ride on the breath. To cut the chant from following the breath, I breathe very fast and if the chant speeds up, I slow it down.

The voice is also not involved. It helps to visualize the chant written down in any language in front of the closed eyes, repeatedly. Let the chant stop, and to go deeper into the practice, we can do some mental arithmetic and place the chant right when the answer is reached in the mind; in that exact place, so to speak.

Think of the number 7, add 20, divide by 9, minus 2. Chant.

Allow the chant to drop. If there was a deeper absorption, it means that the exercise was successful. Watch the spaces between the chants as you listen to the recording. Pick up the chant mentally as soon as the chanting stops. *Oṃ namaḥ śivāya*.

Stop the chant one more time. Watch the spaces between, and then chant as soon as the chants stops. *Oṃ namaḥ śivāya. Oṃ*

Let the chant stop. Chant-consciousness *is*. No-chant-consciousness *is*. Chant does not disturb consciousness. No chant also does not disturb consciousness.

I am unopposed to silence, unopposed to thought, and unopposed to speech. I am neither rising, nor falling; I am neither gaining, nor losing.

I am *sama,* same, unchanging, always present, here, now, unaffected by anything that happens: *asaṃga*, uninvolved. Let me be able to see this. Let me enjoy being this, at least for today. *Oṃ śāntiḥ śāntiḥ śāntiḥ*.

To access the live session, click HERE or scan the QR code given below:

MEDITATING WITH THE WIND

I take the time to arrive. My connecting to the posture and the life giving breath nourishes the body, and by watching the breath, I am immediately aware that I am awareness itself, *sākṣi*, the witness.

The stillness contrasts with the howling winds that I can hear. Can the sound of the wind bring me back repeatedly to the unmoving, unchanging, center? Can the wind be the *mantra* I focus on? I am free of ups and downs. I am tranquil. I am the indweller of this body, this mind, these senses. I am free of everything around me. Wind comes in spells; it rises, swirls, makes a lot of noise as it goes through the trees and past the buildings, and then it appears to die down. I am the presence that gives the wind its presence. I am the presence that notices the lulls in between. This is *śabdānuviddha savikalpa samādhi*–an absorption using the sounds that are heard.

Each time I hear the wind, it is like chanting the *mantra*. Each time it dies down, it's like the silence between one chant and the next. I practice this starting now. The wind has made it easy for me to meditate. It is doing the job of chanting and manifesting the silence in between also. All I have to do is watch, observe.

Whenever the mind strays, it is as though the wind blows harder, faster and is noisier to bring me back to the *mantra* chanted by *vāyu*. Hearing takes place. The Ear of the ear makes sure that the sound is heard. Sound-consciousness *is*. No-sound-consciousness *is*. Consciousness is unopposed to sound. Consciousness, "I", is unopposed to no sound. Consciousness is unopposed to the hearer. Hearer-consciousness *is*. Unopposed to the heard, heard-consciousness *is;* it is *sat.* Hearer-consciousness is *sat-cit.* Heard-consciousness is also non-different from *sat-cit.* Can I see that I am free being the hearer?

Even when there is nothing in particular to objectify through sound, I still am. I am not dependent on the wind or any other sound for my existence. Subject-consciousness is. Object-consciousness is. Neither subject nor object I am. Consciousness is free of all statuses.

Hearer of the wind, I am. Non separate from the wind, I am. I blow forcefully, whistling as I pass through the tree. I am the tree that bends to receive the wind so that I do not have to break. I am the water that flows. I am the mountain, majestic and tall. I am that consciousness which is all: the hearer, heard, hearing, appearing, manifesting, de-manifesting. Consciousness, I simply am, unopposed to stillness, unopposed to sound, unopposed to hearing. I am free of being the hearer or the heard. Can I retain this stillness as I go about my day? Something to think about. Can I appreciate nature in all her forms? *Oṃ śāntiḥ śāntiḥ śāntiḥ.*

To access the live session, click **HERE** or scan the QR code given below:

NOTHING IS OUTSIDE *ĪŚVARA*

viśvaṃ darpaṇadṛśyamānanagarītulyaṃ nijāntargataṃ
paśyannātmani māyayā bahirivodbhūtaṃ yathā nidrayā
yaḥ sākṣātkurute prabodhasamaye svātmānamevādvayaṃ
tasmai śrīgurumūrtaye nama idaṃ śrīdakṣiṇāmūrtaye

bījasyāntarivāṅkuro jagadidaṃ prāṅnirvikalpaṃ punaḥ
māyākalpitadeśakālakalanāvaicitryacitrīkṛtam
māyāvīva vijṛmbhayatyapi mahāyogīva yaḥ svecchayā
tasmai śrīgurumūrtaye nama idaṃ śrīdakṣiṇāmūrtaye

Idaṃ namaḥ, means "this salutation." Unto whom is this salutation offered? *Īśvara*. Who is this *Īśvara*? What is *Īśvara*? My capacity to see this is *Īśvara*. What *is*, is the Lord, *Īśvara*.The capacity to question what is, also *Īśvara*. My capacity is included in *Īśvara*, *Bhagavān,* Lord. What is this capacity? Where is it located? I can say it is obtained in my mind. I am the witness of this capacity to understand, to see, and to question.

Who is this I? One can say that I am a simple conscious being. I have a location. This conscious being obtained in this body-mind-sense complex. I am conscious of this body, this mind, *prāna*, and the senses. What is *Īśvara*? *Īśvara* is also a conscious being, without a body. I am consciousness with body. *Īśvara* is consciousness, without specific body. All bodies are *Īśvara's* body. *Īśvara* is consciousness without a body, without location; like space, *Īśvara* is all-pervasive, ever present, never absent. Located in this body, I have a specific range, reach. This body is separate from other bodies. All bodies are included in *Īśvara*. My body is included in that consciousness, all-power, all-knowledge, *Īśvara*.

My father's body is also included in *Īśvara*. My mother's body, my mother's mind, her senses are included in *Īśvara*. The body of sister, brother, cousin, aunt, uncle, grandparents are included in *Īśvara*.

With reference to this body that I call mine, I have a specific range. Mother and father are external to me, external to this body-mind complex. A friend is external to me. Siblings, brothers, sisters, cousins, and other relatives are external to me.

The world of names and forms are external from the standpoint of this body, this mind, and these senses; all are external to me. I am consciousness. *Īśvara* is consciousness. My *upādhi* is included in *Bhagavān, Īśvara*. From the standpoint of this *upādhi,* everything is external, but non-separate from *Īśvara*. When I look at myself from the standpoint of identifying with the *upādhi,* I am an individual, helpless, alienated, and separated from everything and everybody.

That is why I can repeatedly help myself by seeing that I am related to the whole, connected. This body made up of five elements is external to me, *adhibhūta*. Are the five elements external to *Īśvara*, to consciousness? Do the five elements exist outside of consciousness? When I think of the five elements, do they exist out of consciousness? Five element consciousness *is*. Body consciousness *is*. What *is*, is *Īśvara*. This is how it is. But why is it like this? That question is *Īśvara*. It is not outside of *I*śvara. I see this, clearly. The mind *is*, the *prāna is*, the *sūkṣma śarīra is,* the subtle body *is*, all is *I*śvara.

The subtle body, comprising the five subtle elements, is not external to *Īśvara*, consciousness. The five subtle elements of my own subtle body are not outside of consciousness, not outside of the total, of *Īśvara*. The individual is included in the total. *Prāna* is not outside of consciousness, *Īśvara*. *Vāyu, adhibhūta* is outside. When I take a deep breath in, it is *adhyātma*, *prāna* is inside and the next time I breathe out, again it is outside. Is *prāna* outside or inside? Is the *vāyu* outside or inside? Is there space inside the pot or is the pot in space?

Adhyātma is inside, centered on me, centered on this body-mind complex, yet not outside *Īśvara*. *Adhibhūta*, that which is external to me, existing as my surroundings, is not outside of *Īśvara*.

What is the connection between *adhyātma* and *adhibhūta*? There is a law that facilitates breathing and various other functions, regulating the subtle exchanges between the outside and the inside. *Adhideva,* a law that connects *adhibhūta* with *adhyātma*, is *Īśvara*, consciousness. Nothing is outside *Īśvara*. My mind is also included in *Īśvara*. The capacity to think is Iśvara. The capacity to conclude is *Īśvara*. The capacity to doubt is *Īśvara*. The capacity to question is *Īśvara*. What I call my emotions, my own emotions, are not outside of *Īśvara*. Sadness is universal. That which is uniform has a pattern, and the reason is *Īśvara*. The capacity to question sadness is *Īśvara*. The drive to overpower this sadness and to see it as an imposter is *Īśvara*.

Sorrow, fear, anger, jealousy, greed, pride, and delusion are not outside of consciousness, *Īśvara*. When I say "my pride", "my delusion", or "my jealousy", I am looking at it from the standpoint of the individual. However, the individual is not outside the total. Seen from the standpoint of the total, they are no longer my emotions. They are included in the vast psychological order. Helplessness, alienation, fear, dissociation, avoidant behavior, depression, anger, and sorrow all have a cause. I can see the cause. It has to do with the connection between a child's background and its reactions to a world that it cannot understand.

What is this world, the parentage, the background? What is this background? It is *Īśvara*. Why I was born? Another vast order, a *kārmic* order. It is *Īśvara*.

Why to this family? *Īśvara*. Order, order of *karma*. Whose *karma?* My own *karma.* Why was I targeted with this *karma*? To think and feel victimized is also the part of the psychological order. The ability to emerge from the victimization is also *Īśvara*.

Can I accept these emotions? Can I accept the *kārmic* order? If I cannot accept them, can I accept my non-acceptance? Can I let go of trying to control the order? Can I be and see the beauty of the order even when it feels inimical to me? Can I see even what feels personally adverse as part of the order?

Hey Bhagavan, let there be less and less of me and more and more of You pervading me, within and without. Less of me means fewer complaints, fewer fears, less resistance, and less sorrow. More of You means more accommodation, more acceptance, and more tranquility. *Oṃ śānti̱ḥ śānti̱ḥ śānti̱ḥ.*

To access the live session, click **HERE** or scan the QR code given below:

SURRENDER TO THE OCEAN OF AUSPICIOUSNESS

I connect to the breath as a way of inhabiting the body, taking the time to arrive. Wherever the mind has been wandering, I gently bring it back to this time, right now, right here, simply by paying attention to the breath. Watching the breath automatically quietens the mind. I pay attention to all the mechanisms of breathing carefully. The belly rises and comes forward with every inhalation. Then I feel the breath in the lungs. I feel the cool air in the nostrils in the in-breath. Then, in the out-breath, the chest relaxes and the belly relaxes, in reverse order from the inhalation. I follow this according to my own breathing pattern.

All is well, I remind myself in this moment. At this time, there is nothing to do, nowhere to go, nothing to gain, nothing to lose, nothing to accomplish, and nothing to demolish. I am free: free to be me. This shift from watching the breath to watching the body is subtle but important to do. I watch the body on my own, part by part, starting with the head all the way to the toes, just watching.

Objectifying the body helps me to see that I am not just this body. I am the indwelling observer. In the same way that I objectify the breath and the body, I can also objectify the senses. Opening the eyes halfway and letting them softly close, I feel the top eyelid touch the bottom eyelid softly, gently. I do this again, half-opening the eyes and softly letting the upper eyelid meet the lower eyelid.

Next, I objectify the sense of touch. The legs touch one another. I can see that. I can feel that. The hands touch one another. The clothes touch the body. The tongue touches the teeth. I wield the sense of touch.

The mind too is an object I can observe. Thoughts come, thoughts go. Thoughts do not have the power to shake me.

Acalaḥ aham, I am unshakable. *Niścalaḥ*, it is the same thing; the changes in the body or the mind cannot shake me. I watch the thoughts without inviting them, chasing after them, or avoiding them. If the mind goes away from watching the thoughts, I gently bring it back, stopping it from running behind the thoughts. Thoughts are like the river; I am on the bank watching the river and how the water flows. Amidst the constant flow of thoughts, the unshakable observer watches. Thoughts come, thoughts go. I am still. I still am. Still I am. Thought is born, thought is, thought is gone. Born, is, gone. Gone, is, born. Born, gone, is. Is, born, gone.

All of this is unfolding on the canvas of now: the timeless I, consciousness. In this mind prepared by watching the thoughts, I can place the *mantra* for *japa* to connect with *Īśvara*. This practice helps me to expand, have focus, and develop staying power, and since it's a mental prayer, I also get *antaḥkaraṇa śuddhi.*

The chant is placed in the mind and repeated without engaging either the voice or the breath. If you find the voice is engaged or the chant is riding on the breath, softly stop the chant and disengage and begin the chant again. As always, the chant distraction happens in between two chants. Watching the space between the chants helps to lessen the distractions.

Oṃ namaḥ śivāya

Unto that which is nothing but auspiciousness, my salutations. Who is this I? The *jīva,* endowed with the body-mind complex, often thinks of herself/himself as inauspicious. The inauspicious one surrenders to the altar of auspiciousness. What remains is only auspiciousness. Begin the chant now.

Allow the chant to stop. Scan the mind and see how the practice is going. Where do I need to firm it up? Where do I need to pay more attention? Start the chant again.

(Chant silently for 1.5 minute)

One more time stop the chant. Scan the body for the posture. Scan the mind. Begin the chant again. (Chant silently for 1 minute)

Stop the chant. Begin again. (Chant silently for 1 minute)

Let the chant stop. If the body and the mind feel more relaxed, it means that the meditation was useful. *Oṃ namaḥ śivāya*

Unto the ocean of auspiciousness, I offer my surrender. What is it that I am surrendering to? To my own notions of being inauspicious, being small, and not mattering. When I surrender my inauspiciousness at the altar of that which is auspiciousness incarnate, there is no more inauspiciousness. It is all consumed in that limitless altar. I am lovable. I am free. I do not need to seek validation from others, at least for today. *Oṃ śānti̱ḥ śānti̱ḥ śānti̱ḥ*.

To access the live session, click **HERE** or scan the QR code given below:

WHAT IS, IS *ĪŚVARA*

When I look at myself from the standpoint of this body, this mind, and these senses, there is a notion of finitude. Not only am I limited from what I am not, but also I feel alienated from the whole. Everything overpowers me, from the smallest bacteria which can cause life threatening illnesses, to the galaxies whose names I do not even know.

There appears to be a separation, a disconnection. What *is* is all one, all non-separate. All that is glorious appears to be far away because I do not include myself in this. First, I have to accept this body as *Īśvara*. I can say at first, it is given by *Īśvara*. Then I can understand it is non-separate from *Īśvara*. The body is non-separate from *Īśvara*, non-separate from the *jagat*.

The earth upon which the body sits, is what makes the body sit in the form of the framework, the bones. The water, which sustains this body, in fact constitutes the major portion of the body in the form of various fluids, blood, endocrine glands, and so on. Whenever I am hungry I am in touch with *agni*, the digestive fire. The fire in the form of hunger is *vaiśvānaraḥ*. I am one with the air each time I breathe. Air enters the lungs, exits the lungs. The space obtaining in this body e.g. between the joints, in the stomach, etc. is non-separate from the space in which the body is, as it were, located.

Never am I away from the *jagat*. *Jagat* is *Īśvara*. Body is *Īśvara*. The connection is very clear. When I see that, if I pollute the air, the water with my own actions, I am the one that suffers from drinking water infused with chemicals and toxins, and suffers from breathing impure air. The conscious being, I, can see this clearly.

Not only there is oneness between this body and the *jagat*, but I can even go and say the *jagat* rises with me and goes to sleep with me. I am consciousness. I am awareness.

The body is part of the *jagat,* yet I am free of the *jagat: a* simple witness, the radiant and self-effulgent I.

Now, the *jagat* is swallowed up; it is non-separate. I am. Non-separate is the *jagat* from me. All that remains is the distance, a perceived distance, between myself and *Īśvara*. The dissimilarities are vast. The ruler is *Īśvara*, ruled am I. The overlord *Īśvara* is, lorded over am I. Powerful *Īśvara* is, limited in power am I. All-pervasive *Īśvara* is, small-pervasive am I. Free of *rāga* and *dveṣa* is *Īśvara,* full of *rāga* and *dveṣa* am I. Erasing these differences is easy because they are not really there.

I have to understand the mind, *ahaṅkāra*, the I-ness, the mineness. That is what comes in the way of enjoying the non-distance, non-separation. That is why I surrender to this altar that is all. This ahaṅkāra has to let go through the medium of *japa*. I chant at first loudly, then a little less loudly, softly, in a whisper, and then mentally for a few rounds.

Oṃ namaḥ Śivāya

I allow the chant to stop, observing the distance between myself and the chant. Chanter *is*, chant *is*. Both are *sat,* both are consciousness. Chant consciousness *is*. What *is*, is *Īśvara*. What *is*, is I, *aham*. Silence-consciousness *is*. I consider the distance between no-chant and I. There is no distance; both are *sat*. No-chant *is*. No-chant-consciousness *is*. Both are *Īśvara,* I. Both are free. *Īśvara* is free of being either.

I transcend the chant. I transcend the silence. I can observe both. I am neither the chant, nor am I the silence. Consciousness is I, consciousness is *Īśvara,* and the as-though bridge for the as-though alienation is *japa*. *Oṃ śāntiḥ śāntiḥ śāntiḥ.*

To access the live session, click **HERE** or scan the QR code given on the next page:

Chant is, chant-consciousness is.
No chant is; no-chant consciousness is

I AM FREE OF THE ROLE, BUT THE ROLE DEPENDS ON ME

I get familiar with the basic person, the meditator. *Dhyātā kaḥ?* Who is the meditator? When I observe the body, I can see that it is inert; it cannot meditate. Neither can the *prāṇa*, nor the mind. Who is the one, who is the *dehi*, not subject to the afflictions of the *deha*? Who is the one that dwells in this body, a flawed body, finite, full of shortcomings, yet free of all blemishes, all shortcomings? Who is this conscious being?

To claim this conscious being as I is effortless. One can easily see that one is not the body-mind complex. One is the inhabiter of this assemblage called the body, called the mind, called the senses, the *prāṇa,* and so on.

How do I connect with the basic person? By seeing myself as the observer, *sākṣī* of the body, of the mind, of the senses, of everything. How well do I know this *sākṣī*? The role of the *sākṣī* becomes invisible in and through all the roles I have to play.

I take the time now to see myself as free of all roles. A son, a daughter, are both superimpositions upon that consciousness which is inherently free of that superimposition. Student, again, is a superimposition upon that consciousness which is free of that role. Sibling. See the truth of this role also.

Employer, employee, whatever is applicable, see the truth of that role. And then again, if applicable, consider this for the roles of spouse, father, mother or any other roles that you play. I am free of the role, but the role depends on me for its very being, its very execution.

The role is not permanent. The designation of "son" and "daughter" are impermanent. Even on the everyday level, roles cease to be when I sleep. There is no role in sleep.

There is no son, no daughter, no sister, no brother, no friend, no employee, no employer, no spouse, no mother, no father, no home owner, no business person, no engineer, no doctor, no graphic artist or any other occupation you can think of. All are gone in sleep. Only I remain. I am not gone.

I am that Truth that neither comes nor goes. I am here to stay. I am the canvas, vast and free, upon which all these roles play themselves out, like so many small video clips: the identification of being a son or daughter, bringing with the role care and love no doubt, but also perhaps feelings of guilt, hurt, and lack.

It's a movie. I am the audience. I am not in the movie. I am the screen, blank, pure, and free. The movie being played on the screen does not affect the screen. If there is a fire in the movie, the screen does not get burnt.

nainaṅ chindanti śastrāṇi nainaṅ dahati pāvakaḥ

That which cannot be affected by any of the five elements, *aham, sākṣī, cetā,* a sentient being in whose presence everything unfolds.

Every day so many video clips of ecstasy and agony, guilt and hurt, play in the movies like shadow and light. *Rāga-dveṣas* are the main characters in the movie. They chase each other and want to be fulfilled. My own omissions and commissions are also characters in this movie, a *saṃsāra* movie.

I do not feature in this film. I am in the audience, just being, just watching. My omissions and commissions are characters in the movie. Why did I do this? Why did I not do this? Why did somebody else do this to me? Why did somebody else not do this to me? These regrets are characters in the movie, *chāyātapau,* the show of shadow and light. It is like a shadow puppet dance. The shadow puppet show also needs light.

I am that light which makes the show go on. The light is not part of the show. The light simply reveals the show.

Anger, jealousy, pain, fear, and depression are all cameo characters. They have special guest appearances. I can see them as various emotions personified in film, fighting each other, destroying each other, *namaḥ*.

I am free of all this drama. Sometimes the movie is a comedy. The antics of a *saṃsārī* starring in the movie makes one laugh. Trying to make the finite into infinite is indeed a joke. Sometimes it is a tragedy. From start to finish, all the characters weep. Sometimes it's a little bit of both, laughing and crying.

If I participated in all of this, I would just go mad. That is why it is important to see myself as free, the basic person, conscious being. The problems of the roles cannot touch me. The role is dependent on me, but I am free of the role. Problems belong to the roles, but not to the self-effulgent I, who is free, full, forever *sākṣī*.

Now, I can ask this meditator to connect to *Bhagavān* in the form of *japa, Oṃ namaḥ śivāya*

Watch the spaces between the chants as I chant and pick up the chant mentally as soon as I stop.

Oṃ namaḥ śivāya

Oṃ

Let the chant stop. Notice the inner space between oneself and the roles. If you are comfortable being who you are, acknowledge it in so many words. It is effortless to be free. It is effortless to be me.

It is effortless to have an open heart and to be an accommodating, non-demanding, non-judgmental, contented, compassionate, and objective person. This is the Truth of who I am. May I see it! May I live it! *Oṃ śāntiḥ śāntiḥ śāntiḥ*.

To access the live session, click **HERE** or scan the QR code given below:

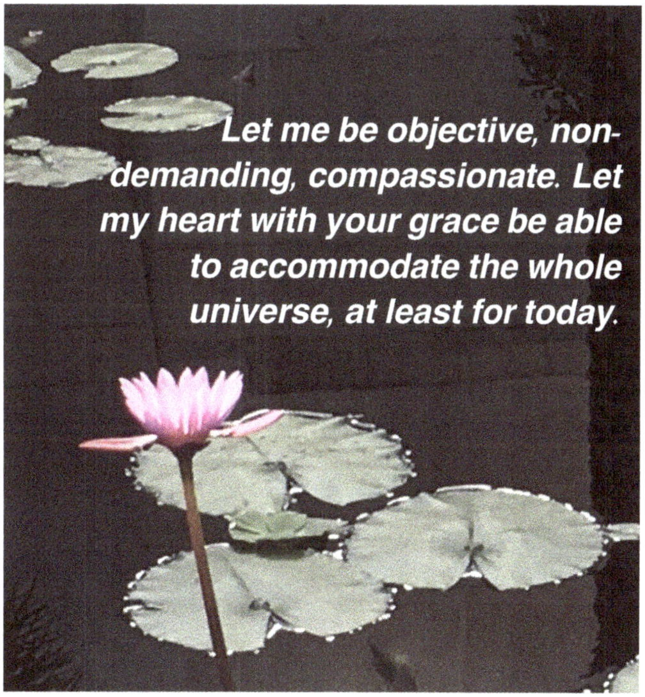

I AM THE WITNESS CONSCIOUSNESS

viśvaṃ darpaṇadṛśyamānanagarītulyaṃ nijāntargataṃ
paśyannātmani māyayā bahirivodbhūtaṃ yathā nidrayā
yaḥ sākṣātkurute prabodhasamaye svātmānamevādvayaṃ
tasmai śrīgurumūrtaye nama idaṃ śrīdakṣiṇāmūrtaye

bījasyāntarivāṅkuro jagadidaṃ prāṅnirvikalpaṃ punaḥ
māyākalpitadeśakālakalanāvaicitryacitrīkṛtam
māyāvīva vijṛmbhayatyapi mahāyogīva yaḥ svecchayā
tasmai śrīgurumūrtaye nama idaṃ śrīdakṣiṇāmūrtaye

The *jagat* is like a city in the mirror. A mirror that is fixed, let's say, in a busy market, high up, somewhere where it reflects the whole city. In the city there is traffic honking, people going about their day to school, the office, and elsewhere. At the market, shopping, buying, selling, and all kinds of transactions are taking place, all reflected in the mirror. A very busy city scenario one can visualize, crowded with events, people, goings and comings. There are also animals in the city, and other stationary things like mountains and trees.

Carācarātmakam jagata, reflected in the mirror. *Carācarātmikā nagarī*, city reflected in the mirror, comprising sentient, insentient, moving, and unmoving things.

The stress of the city, with the people going and coming does not touch the mirror. The pollution of the traffic hanging in the air also does not touch or affect the mirror. Now in the city, if there is lightning, thunder, it does not affect the mirror. It simply reflects the reflecting witness, the inner witness. Now I can visualize that when it is raining in the city, the mirror does not get wet.

darpaṇadṛśyamānanagarī, viśvaṃ, darpaṇadṛśyamānanagarītulyaṃ, this *jagat* likewise, seen, acknowledged, cognized in the heart is like the city in the mirror.

Nijāntargataṃ, in one's own heart, this *jagat* is, this city is.

Ātmani paśyan, seeing this within oneself.

Bahirivodbhūtaṃ, as though projected outside.

Like even in the dream state, *yathā nidrayā.*

In the dream state, many things are seen: a dream sunrise, dream river, dream bodies, dream sky, dream earth, dream plants, dream people, dream animals, dream I. I too have a body in the dream: a dream mind, dream sense organs. I am one with the dream that I project. I identify with the dream. When dream happiness comes, I am elated. When dream sorrow comes, I am *duḥkhī,* dejected. Where is this dream happening? Within, *paśyannātmani.* But during dreamtime it looks to be an intact outer *jagat:* real, palpable, and separate from me, the dreamer. I revel, I rejoice. In the next minute I cry, I fight, I am afraid, I am angry; I feel dream emotions. To me they seem real because I do not know I am dreaming. Dream time for me is real time. The dream world is the real world.

viśvaṃ darpaṇadṛśyamānanagarītulyaṃ
bahirivodbhūtaṃ yathā nidrayā
As though the world is projected outside, in the dream state, I engage. The dream world is exactly like the world I live in, with the same people, traffic, animals, and activities. I awaken slowly from this dream. It takes me a few seconds to orient myself to understand that there was no dejection, no rejection, no tears, no fears. It was all a dream. No traffic, no cars, no people. Just me. My memory, my desire spun this *jagat,* this dream *jagat.*

Who is it that woke up from the dream? Who is this I that finally understood this is a dream? We can say the I is the conscious being. What is it that made me see that this is a dream? It was awareness, consciousness, invariable presence in the dream, as the dream, that never became the dream. I am that consciousness.

Now I am awake firmly in the waking world as the waker. I am conscious of my surroundings, of the *jagat* outside. There are people, cars, sky, rain, sunshine, various activities and pursuits belonging to me, belonging to others. All are real because earlier what I saw was the dream. This is the reality. If this is the reality, where does the *jagat* go in sleep? If the *jagat* sleeps when I am asleep, we cannot say it always *is*.

Therefore the example of the city in the mirror is very helpful. I am the witness consciousness, witnessing the waking state. I am neither waker, nor dreamer, nor the sleeping person. I simply *am*. The witness of the waking and dreaming states. In sleep I am that consciousness where there is nothing to witness. The waking state is also dreamlike, comes, goes, displaced by the dreaming state, by the sleeping state.

viśvaṃ darpaṇadṛśyamānanagarītulyaṃ nijāntargataṃ
paśyannātmani māyayā bahirivodbhūtaṃ yathā nidrayā
māyayā udbhūtaṃ

The city in the dream is due to *māyā, avidyā* of the *jīva* that projects memories and desires and takes them to be real. A city in the waking state is also a projection, *Īśvara's* projection, again due to *māyā:* this time, an all-knowledge aspect of *māyā.*

Unto that Lord whose grace wakes me up from this nightmare of thinking the *jagat* to be real, *namaḥ,* my surrender, my salutations.

Idam namaḥ, this surrender, right now, right here, is unto whom? *Yaḥ sākṣātkurute,* the one who makes it clear through teaching.

Prabodhasamaye, makes me wake up from this nightmare of thinking the *jagat* to be real. What is this teaching? *Sarvam svātmānamevādvayaṃ,* all this is myself alone, *sat-cit-ānanda. Tasmai śrīgurumūrtaye,* unto this embodiment of the *guru,* who takes away *ajñānam, idam namaḥ,* this salutation. *Tasmai namaḥ,* unto this *Dakṣiṇāmūrti,* who banishes *saṃsāra* within my head, *namaḥ,* by showing me that I am the non-dual Self in and through the various states - waking, dreaming, sleeping, *namaḥ. tasmai namaḥ, idam namaḥ, tasmai namaḥ, idam namaḥ. Oṃ śāntiḥ śāntiḥ śāntiḥ.*

To access the live session, click **HERE** or scan the QR code given below:

I AM AT HOME WITH MYSELF

I firm up the posture with the head, neck, and back in a single, straight line, closing the eyes softly. I clasp the hands on the lap, with the fingers touching, taking the time to arrive and to connect to the breath.

I tell myself as I breathe in, I take the time to arrive. Breathing out, I tell myself I am home. Breathing in, I take the time to arrive. Breathing out, I am home. Breathing in, I have arrived. Breathing out, I am home. Breathing in, I am aware of this body. Breathing out, I allow it to rest. Breathing in, I am aware of my body. Breathing out, I allow it to stop, to rest.

The whole day I am running from one thing to another. My whole life I am running, striving, and reaching. Now, I authorize my body to stop. Just breathing in and breathing out mindfully helps the body to let go. The movements of the body–running, striving and other expressions of restlessness– are because of habit. Maybe I learned it from the parents. Maybe they learned it from their parents. Maybe I learned it from everyone around me. Now, it is time to change the habit of running, striving, and reaching. I direct the body to stop, to rest deeply with the help of the breath. Breathing in, I have arrived. Breathing out, I am home.

With the practice of learning to sit comfortably and to enjoy sitting, new vistas open for me. When I am quiet, I can tune into a different kind of music. My lungs play a rhythmic music with every in-breath, with every out-breath, softly. I enjoy listening to the music of the lungs, subtle sounds of the breath that again encourage the body and the mind to stop running, and to just be.

Then, when I look deeper, I find that the heart is also making music: the drum beats of life. When I stop running, I can enjoy the music of the heart, the music of the breath. Breathing in, "I have arrived." Breathing out, "this is my home." I am at home.

The mind and the body are connected. When I will the body to stop and watch my breath, the mind also becomes quiet, tranquil. Breathing in, I observe the mind. Breathing out, I let it sink into my heart. Breathing in, I watch the mind. Breathing out, I let it stay with my heart.

When I run towards something or when I keep running away from something, there is a hardness in my life. Learning to sit mindfully takes away the hardness in the body, in the mind. The hardness of striving, catching, and conquering softens.

Breathing in, I soften the face, the brows, and the forehead, like the Buddha in meditation. Once again, breathing in, I soften the face. Breathing out, I let go of all that does not belong. I soften the eyebrows. The eyelids are softly closed and as I breathe softly I make sure that the face is soft; the cheeks are soft, the chin is soft. The jaws are soft, not tightly clenched. The tongue is soft and heavy in between the teeth. Soft is the torso. The stomach and abdomen too are soft. Soft is my inward gaze. There is nowhere to go, nothing to do, nothing to achieve, and nothing to lose. All is soft and free.

When I watch the mind also, I let the thoughts softly fall in the mind: soundless thoughts, soft thoughts, softly falling in the mind. I am the sākṣī whose nature is soft. The one that does not run away is the *sākṣī*, the truth of the I. Soft is the gaze, inward gaze. Soft is the object of the *vikṣaṇam* of the gaze. Soft thoughts, softly falling in the mind. Softly watched by me the *sākṣī.*

I am home. That is when I can stop running, when I come home. When I am at home, I see that it is a place of rest. There is nowhere to go and nothing to do for this ragged *jīva* who is tired of running, tired of striving, tired of doing, and tired of being a doer.

When I am at home I can relax. Sweet is this sense of homecoming after a long hard day of work. The internal homecoming likewise is also sweet, even more welcome after lifetimes of running, striving after empty pursuits, chasing rainbows and dead ends, only to start all over again. Again I run, again I strive, again I grab, again I conquer. There is finite gain and then there is loss. Life after life of running makes me a tired *jīva*. I don't know when to stop. I don't know how to stop.

Now I can see that when I will the body to stop and rest, the mind connected to the body also stops. They are interconnected. In the same way, when I train the mind to stop, the body also lets go. I am finally home. When I stop, I can see that I have arrived. In order to enjoy being home in this *antaḥkaraṇa*, the body and the mind have to stop. I have to learn to let go of striving, of control, of drama.

Śrī Krishna Govinda hare Murārī, hey Nātha Nārāyaṇa Vāsudeva

I can practice putting a full stop after every thought. There is no more argument, no more strife, for I am home. What do I need to come home? I need a mind that is well lit, nicely ventilated, and free of the dampness of resentment by letting in a lot of light: the sunshine of *sākṣīta*, observing. Ventilation comes as the cool breeze of *śamā*, accommodation. The mind must benefit from the fresh air of a clear *buddhi* with proper thinking, and precise discernment. The home must not be a scary place; it should be welcoming. It must be a place where the fears are surrendered to *Bhagavān*.

Hey Nātha Nārāyaṇa Vāsudeva

A home is a place that is familiar. The more I take the time to know this non-striving, non-running person, the more I am in familiar terrain. Home is a place of love for myself and the universe. When the eclipse of hurts and guilt is removed, all that is there is love.

Śrī Krishna Govinda hare Murārī

May Lord Krishna slay the inner demons of all the things I do not want in this home: the anger, the fear, jealousy, delusion, and *ajñānam*. May it all go.

hey Nātha Nārāyaṇa Vāsudeva

I am at home because there is nowhere I would rather be. I am at home because whatever I want is right here, right now. It's centered on me. There is nowhere to go, nothing to do, nothing to gain, and nothing to lose. I am free. I am whole. I am just me. Breathing in, I have arrived. Breathing out, I am at home with myself. *Oṃ śānti̱ḥ śānti̱ḥ śānti̱ḥ*.

To access the live session, click **HERE** or scan the QR code given below:

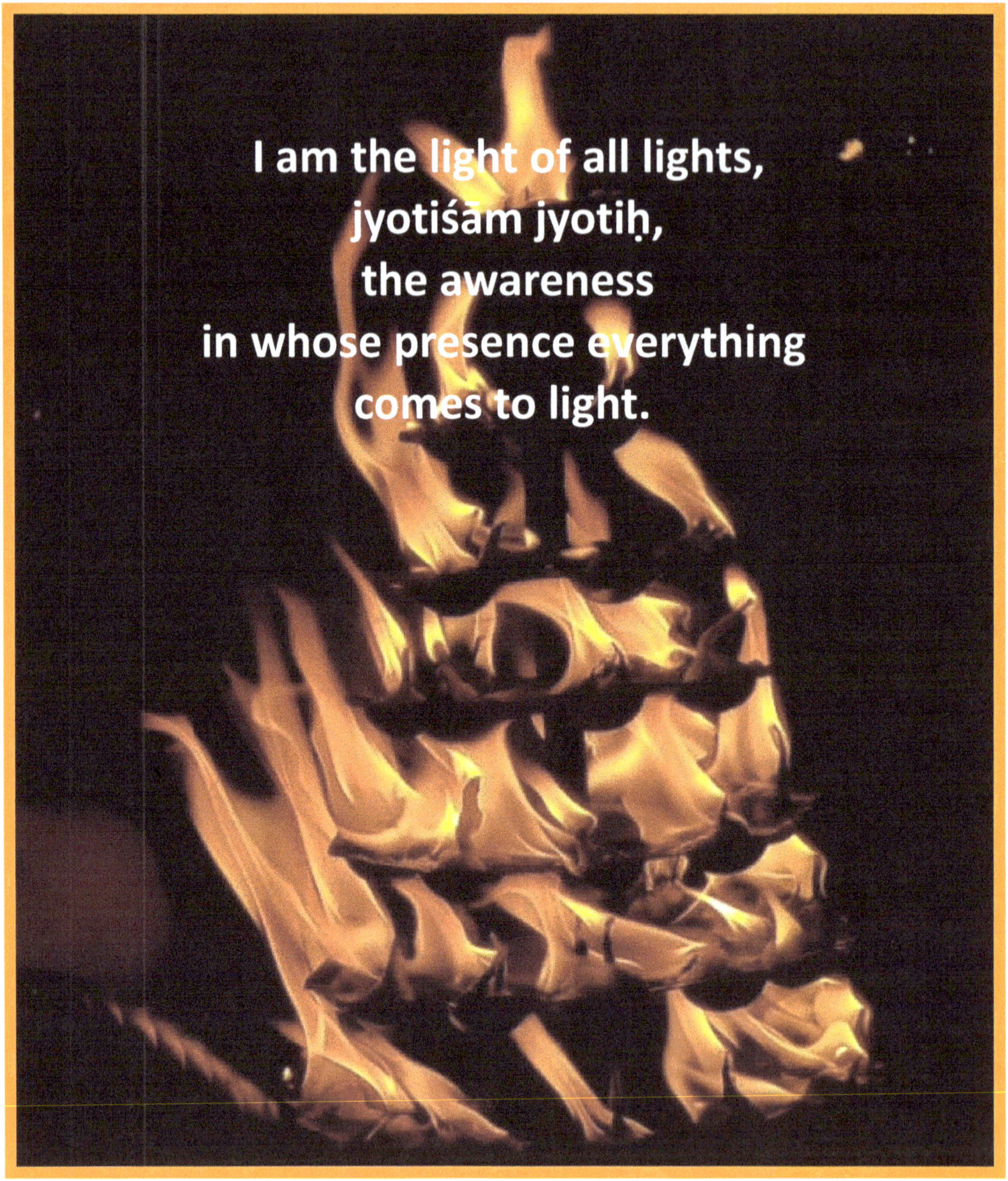
I am the light of all lights,
jyotiśām jyotiḥ,
the awareness
in whose presence everything
comes to light.

SECTION III

Quick Meditations for Busy People

I am the presence that moves
I am the air that I breathe
I am the bird, I am its flight
in the vast breadth of the sky
I am in everything
that is set to sway
I am in all that is meant to stay
all is in order when I say
"Things as-though come
and then go away."

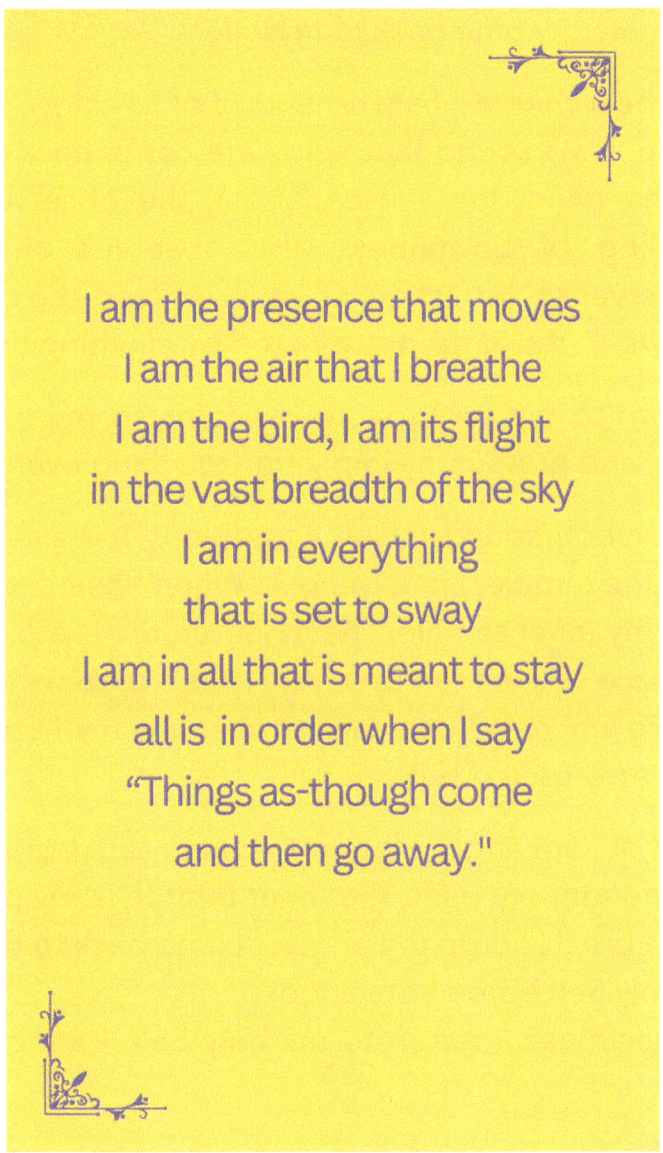

BEING ONESELF

The bell is an invitation to come back to myself. Whether I am scattered, whether I am lost, whether I am angry, whether I am stressed, whether I am sad, the bell reminds me it is time to come back to myself.

I am letting go. When I hear the bell, I am reminded of its clarity, which is my own clarity. It's a sound of invitation. It's a sound that helps me come back to myself. What is this "myself"? The body, the mind, the senses, and I, the observer of all of them. The observer of this feeling of unwellness, the observer of emotions that seem uncontrollable, the observer of distraction, of anger, of fear. The observer is not affected. Who is this observer? The 'I', the *ātmā*, not affected by anything that I observe.

Hearing the bell, I return to my *swarupa*, to my form, to my nature. Like the bell, my nature is clear, pleasant, and profoundly impactful, touching everything around it.

The sound of the bell is a holy sound. In some traditions, it is a call to prayer. The temple has bells. When I go to the temple, I ring the bell. When I hear the bell in the meditation, it's an invitation to visit my inner temple. The inner temple is a place of calm. It is safe. It is not crowded. It is a place where I can be myself. It is a place where no one can hurt me or affect me. It is a place where no one can get me. It is my home. It is me. The sacred bell invites me to inhabit my sacred self.

In the temple, I forget that I am angry. I forget that I am sad. Instead, I am in awe. I am in a place where I can surrender my pain. The inner temple is my place of refuge, where I can go anytime I need a break. I drop the anger. I come back to the temple. I come back to my sacred Self. My holy Self is free from anger.
I drop the fear, the insecurities. I return to my holy Self. I am completely safe, sound, secure, and unafraid.

The holy Self is *Īśvara*, the ultimate observer. I drop my frustration. I come back to the holy Self, who is free of frustration. I am holy. Frustration comes, frustration goes. The one who watches the frustration is free of frustration.

When I hear the bell, I drop my sorrow. All sadness is dissolved by the sound of this powerful invitation to visit my inner temple where I am free of sorrow and safe with myself. I am comfortable with myself. I am free with myself. I love being with myself. I love being myself.

The bell is an invitation to, and a recognition of, homecoming. I am home. I am at home with myself. *Oṃ śāntiḥ śāntiḥ śāntiḥ*.

To access the live session, click **HERE** or scan the QR code given below:

RELIEVING STRESS

I allow the bell to lead me back to myself to spend a few minutes in meditation before starting my day. But wait, I don't have time to meditate. There is so much I have to do. I'm already late. The deadlines are piling up along with my stress. Reason and logic tell me, don't continue to sit here and listen to this. Get up, leave the house, get in the car, go about your day. What is this short practice going to do for you anyway? You have been like this all your life: a ball of stress. You unwind a bit, and then it all comes back. Who are you trying to kid?

Meditation is for those who are contemplative by nature, who are calm. That's not me. I'm a doer. I'm on the go. I get restless, when I sit. I feel upset. Everything I have worked hard to achieve seems to be hanging on a thread. I don't have time. I am busy. I'm responsible for so many people, so many projects, so many things. I can't take the time. This is what reasoning says. This is the monologue of logic.

Yet, there is a small candlelight of hope. Somewhere in the depths there lies a hope for a miracle because that's what it's going to take, to overcome this stress. A hope that somehow everything that has been wrong throughout this life will be righted. In the course of these few minutes, I succumb to the hope, I succumb to the call of this hope, the call of the bell. The lamp grows a little brighter. The sound of the bell peals a little louder. My shoulders come down several inches. They do not hug my ears. I'm helpless when faced with this stress. I recognize the helplessness and I pray; that is the only thing to do when one is helpless, but I do not have time to pray. Things are waiting for me: I'm late for work, late for things to do. The outer deadlines become inner pressures, or rather, the outer deadlines trigger inner pressures and bring them to the forefront of my mind.

I don't have time to chant a hundred and eight names, a thousand and eight names. I don't have time to compose eloquent songs, stanzas in praise. O Lord, the All -Pervasive

One, I do not even have time to set up an altar for you, except bow to what is already there in my heart.

śrīrāma rāma rāmeti rame rāme manorame,
sahasranāma tattulyaṃ rāma nāma varānane.
rāmanāma varānana oṃ nama iti

The heart beats slower. The heart beats more slowly. The tension is skimmed off the consciousness. My awareness is free. I do not identify with the stress. Things to do, places to go, people to see, appointments to keep... none of this can happen without keeping an appointment with myself. The bell is the indication that the most important appointment has begun: time for me. Time for me is time for *Īśvara*. Time with myself is time with *Īśvara*.

O Goddess Lalita, the playful one, teach me how to play. Teach me how to make work into play, by consciously dis-identifying with everything I have to do by knowing that you are the *kartri*, the doer. Make me an instrument of your doing. I put my life and all its endeavors in your great lap. I relinquish all the deadlines, all the projects, the activities. I relinquish also onto your lap my imperfections, my annoyances, my fears, my insecurities. Take them, O Lalitā, mother Goddess, the playful one. Free me from myself, from the grip of this stress, this anxiety. I pray to you, O Goddess Lalitā, don't abandon me at my time of need. It is difficult for me to sit and make time to pray. I do not know how, Help me now, O Mother Goddess, Divine Mother. I seek refuge in you. Take away the pain, the anxiety, the fear connected to my loved ones. Let me have the wisdom. Touch me with the sword of your discrimination so that I know that everything has its own karma, that all is well. That everyone I love, including my animals, the people, my children, have their path in you. They follow their path safely. They do what is to be done, enveloped by your gentle direction.

I put my loved ones in your lap, O Mother Goddess of beauty and grace. I put my children in your lap. They are given to you by me. They are really yours. They belong to you. Take care of them. May they not come to harm. I put the elders in my life in your lap. My worries about their wellbeing, I dedicate unto you. All the stress connected to this body, this mind, my fears - connected to my health, my worries about growing old, I put in your lap.

O Mother, free me from the hold of this anxiety. My own mind is tangled, confused, afraid... fraught with indecision, anger, and anxiety; this bundle of nerves, I place in your lap. May your graceful glance untangle these sorrows, and worries, none of which I can control. O mother Lalita, teach me how to play. Bring back humor, bring back your light, bring back your lightness. Let everything I do be infused with playfulness, and effortlessness, imbued with the knowledge that it is your doing, not mine. That you will take care of the deadlines, the traffic, the offspring, the significant other, the elders, the young ones, fears about the environment, fears about the world, the pain of the world. I give unto you, I give back to you.

Give me the inner space to be able to observe this anxiety. Give me the tools to let it go, just by the thought of you. Let all my work be play, be playful. Let me be childlike, knowing that I am secure with all my worries consigned to your lap. Let my breathing be deep. Let me feel safe. Let me be free of worry. Let me be free of stress. Let me be free of anxiety. Let me be free above all of needing to control everything. Let me understand that there is nothing in my hand. Let me learn to let go.
The more I let go, the more I can sense your lightness. The more I let go, the more I am free. Teach me to witness my stress, to be a *sākṣī*. Teach me that whatever I can observe is not me. May the bell be your voice, your sound, your invitation to come home to myself, to come home to my inner temple, safe and free, safe and free of anxiety.

All is well. All is play. Work is play, work is playfully done. Drive is play. Sitting in traffic is play. Deadlines, play. Worries, play. Abide in me, O Mother. Teach me. Enlighten me. Lighten my burdens. *Oṃ śāntiḥ śāntiḥ śāntiḥ.*

To access the live session, click **HERE** or scan the QR code given below:

DECISION MAKING

Oṃ bhūrbhuvaḥ svaḥ tatsaviturvareṇyaṃ bhargo
devasya dhīmahi dhiyo yo naḥ pracodayāt

My posture is steady. I am not slouching. The head, neck, and back are in a single straight line. The eyes are softly closed. I find that there are so many choices that I have to make in the course of a day, in the course of my life. Sometimes I get confused. I don't know what to pick.

Each thing seems correct and then it seems wrong. In the grip of this uncertainty, I find that it is very difficult to lead my life. Because the choices I make impact not only myself, but others as well. Someone is happy with my choice, someone is not. And if most people are happy, it doesn't seem to be the right thing for me.

The uncertainty stops me from trying to do my best. I find that I cannot do my best. I cannot perform. I have anxiety. Anxiety of always negotiating people's moods, anger, displeasure. Anxiety of making a mistake, Anxiety of being wrong, doing something wrong. Anxiety connected with embarrassment. My stomach ties itself up in knots.

O mother Gayatri- the mother, who gives me discrimination, have mercy upon me, your child. O Goddess Gayatri, I surrender unto you my indecision. I know not where to go. I know not what to choose anymore. I'm caught in the web of anxieties, my own and those belonging to others. I know what is correct, but sometimes that knowing is shadowed by pressures, my own and others.

O Goddess, you who are in the form of knowledge, you who shine like the sun, your brightness is like the effulgence of the Sun. In fact, your brightness gives the Sun its light. Sit in my mind, O Gayatri. I invoke you, I invite you to sit in my heart, in my mind.

Supervise the choices that I make with the gentleness that I know to be you, with motherly compassion, devoid of judgment.

I invite you into my heart, O Mother Gayatri, O Goddess, O great Goddess of the Vedas. I gently wash your feet as a sign of welcome, as a sign of accepting you, the discrimination you have to offer me in my life.

I offer you now water to drink, O mother. May you quench your thirst and in the process may my uncertainty be quenched as well.

I bathe your form, O Mother, with all the choicest of things: milk, honey, yogurt, water, and fruits. May they nourish me. May all the *dravyas*, the things with which I bathe your form, nourish my capacity to make the right choices.

O Mother Goddess Gayatri, I offer you clothes. May I be garbed in the right choices. May I wear my choices proudly without hesitation or uncertainty.

I now offer you flowers. May each flower that falls on your form, on your feet, be one more resolve by which I may overcome and be healed of my indecision.

Oṃ bhūrbhuvaḥ svaḥ tatsaviturvareṇyaṃ bhargo devasya dhīmahi dhiyo yo naḥ pracodayāt

O Mother, we as a humanity lack clarity, and as a result have made bad decisions that impact the collective life and the planet. Heal us from the effects of these decisions and the addictions that we seem to have cultivated to wrong decisions.

I offer you the incense stick. May its fragrance waft far and wide and be a reminder to all to seek refuge in you for making the right choices. I offer you some sweet rice as *naivedyam*, the ritual offering. May I partake of the sweetness of dharma in my life. May I partake of the sweetness of right conduct, right living. May the toxins of wrong desires leave me as I'm filled with the sweetness that is you. May the toxins of wrong desires leave humanity. May all our minds be in tune with what is correct, with what is right. May I never swerve from my duty. May all of us never swerve from our duties.

O Mother Goddess Gāyatrī, I wave the *āratī* in front of you - a camphor lamp filled with the alive flame. May this flame enter my heart, my mind, guide my discrimination, guide my choices. May this flame burn to ashes all residues of resistance to doing what is correct. May all my fear in treading the correct path be reduced to ashes. May my hesitation disappear in the light of this flame. May the correct choices be lit up as even your form in me.

Mother, you are all I have that separates me from the correct and the wrong. Between the right and the wrong, you sit at the crossroads. Please direct me on the correct path. No matter how thorny, no matter how hard, may I seek this correctness.

May I not take the low road. May I not take needless shortcuts that in the long run turn out to be not shortcuts at all. May we all follow the high road. May we all make the right choices. Impel our minds, O Mother Goddess. Abide in me.
May you always abide in me. May I seek refuge in you. May I abide in you. May you abide in me. *Oṃ śāntiḥ śāntiḥ śāntiḥ*.

To access the live session, click **HERE** or scan the QR code given below:

Amidst the constant flow of thoughts, the unshakable observer watches. Thoughts are like ripples, they come and go. I am still. Thought is born, thought is, thought is gone. I am still; I still am.

MEDITATION ON ANGER

Oṃ Namo Bhagavate Rudrāya
Unto *bhagavān Rudrā*, my salutations, *namaḥ*

A meditation upon anger. I sit comfortably. My head, neck and shoulders are in a single line, in alignment with the spine. My eyes are softly closed.

O Lord Rudra, I succumb to my anger. It overpowers me, brandishes me about, throwing me in situations that I do not want to be in, tearing me up from inside. When I'm angry, I lose clarity, I lose my reasoning. I'm afraid. I'm afraid of hurting myself or hurting someone else I love.

I know not where this anger comes from. I only know I am in the grip of it. I cannot seem to plan its arrival or to anticipate it. I just know that it is upon me and there is nothing I can do except watch it ravage me like a tornado, leaving residues of its existence in and around me long after it has passed. I keep spending my life rebuilding and repairing after bouts of anger, undoing the damage they cause in myself and in those around me.

Help me, O Lord Rudra, to get understanding, clarity, to learn how to manage my anger. May I understand that anger is a manifestation of you. It is your creation, not mine. May I learn to use your creation responsibly. May I understand the dangers of anger, in the way it limits how productive and functional I can be, in how devoted I can be to you, to my spiritual growth, and to my emotional maturity.

Give me the tools to manage my anger. Help me to understand that anger is nothing but thwarted desire. I did not get my way and I am angry. I did not get what I want, I am angry. I got what I did not want, I am angry.

Give me the discrimination to be able to see that. Nothing and no one has the power to make me angry, except my own desires that run like wild horses.

Give me, grant me the reins of discrimination to hold these desires in check. Not by suppressing them, but by letting them go, managing them with discrimination, with my *buddhi*, my intelligence.

Let me have the ability to choose from which desires I seek to fulfill and which I let go as fancies arising in the mind. Even as they arise, I offer them unto you as I say *namaḥ*.

Let me understand that anger is not needed as a transactional force in the everyday world. I can get things done without being angry. I can have relationships with people without subjecting them or targeting them to my anger.
Give me your grace O Lord Rudra to see my desires through *dharma*, to filter my desires through what is correct. Let all the desires not in keeping with *dharma* be crushed by your gaze, by your grace.

Let me learn not to resist what is correct. Let me learn to flow with the river of *dharma*, to be in the flow of *dharma*. Let her cool waters console me. Let the flow make me a person who is in alignment with thoughts, words and deeds.

Let all the unkempt desires be flooded by the deluge of *dhārmik* living. Let them be engulfed, healed, immersed in the flow of *dharma*. Let me sense this flow in me. Let *dharma* flow along with the blood in my veins and arteries.

May I be one incapable of going against dharma, against what is correct. Let my *rāga-dveṣas*, my likes and dislikes, subside alongside my anger. Purify me, O Lord *Rudrā*, with the power of your gaze. May I be free from being subject to my anger, from subjecting others to my anger. *Oṃ śāntiḥ śāntiḥ śāntiḥ*.

To access the live session, click **HERE** or scan the QR code given below:

RECONNECTING WITH ONESELF

Making a space to come home, to oneself that is what is called *dhyāna* in Sanskrit, meditation. A connection to *Īśvara*, a connection to God, a connection to *Bhagavān* - the one whose laws affect me, my emotions, my body, my mind, my efforts and the results thereof.

Hey Īśvara, O God, I am having a bad day today. Nothing seems to be going as I would like it to. Nothing is going my way. Despite my best efforts to be happy, to be cheerful, to enjoy life, I find myself lagging behind. It is almost as it were, something has overpowered me. I cannot get out from under the grip of these strong emotions.

I feel alone, unloved, abandoned, left to my own devices. Constantly misunderstood. I feel afraid. I cannot seem to console myself and I do not know to whom to turn. I tell myself - I am grown up now, I should be able to handle this. Yet, all reasoning, all logic seems to vanish when I am in the grip of these powerful and negative emotions.

Śivā - the auspicious one, *namaḥ* - my surrender to you. You, who was able to swallow the poison of the universe make me free from the grip of these toxic emotions. I lay them at your feet with every chant of *Oṃ namaḥ Śivāya*.

Oṃ namaḥ Śivāya, Oṃ namaḥ Śivāya, Oṃ namaḥ Śivāya, I surrender.

Oṃ namaḥ Śivāya, Oṃ namaḥ Śivāya, Oṃ namaḥ Śivāya, Oṃ namaḥ Śivāya, I let go of this burden. I can't carry it any longer.

Oṃ namaḥ Śivāya, Oṃ namaḥ Śivāya, Oṃ namaḥ Śivāya, Oṃ namaḥ Śivāya, help me Lord *Śivā*.

Oṃ namaḥ Śivāya, Oṃ namaḥ Śivāya, Oṃ namaḥ Śivāya, Oṃ namaḥ Śivāya, Oṃ namaḥ Śivāya, there is no one other than you.

Oṃ namaḥ Śivāya, Oṃ namaḥ Śivāya, Oṃ namaḥ Śivāya, Oṃ namaḥ Śivāya, I let go. I focus.

Oṃ namaḥ Śivāya, Oṃ namaḥ Śivāya, Oṃ namaḥ Śivāya, hara hara, take away, take away, take away everything that I do not want in this life. Take away these feelings, now.

Oṃ namaḥ Śivāya, Oṃ namaḥ Śivāya, Oṃ namaḥ Śivāya, Oṃ namaḥ Śivāya, Oṃ namaḥ Śivāya, Oṃ namaḥ Śivāya, Oṃ namaḥ Śivāya, Oṃ namaḥ Śivāya, Oṃ namaḥ Śivāya, all there is, is you. Let me disappear, let there just be you.

Oṃ namaḥ Śivāya, Oṃ namaḥ Śivāya, Oṃ namaḥ Śivāya, Oṃ namaḥ Śivāya, Oṃ namaḥ Śivāya, Oṃ namaḥ Śivāya, Oṃ namaḥ Śivāya, Oṃ namaḥ Śivāya, Oṃ namaḥ Śivāya, I bathe you with my sorrow.

Oṃ namaḥ Śivāya, Oṃ namaḥ Śivāya, Oṃ namaḥ Śivāya, Oṃ namaḥ Śivāya, Oṃ namaḥ Śivāya, Oṃ namaḥ Śivāya, Oṃ namaḥ Śivāya, Oṃ namaḥ Śivāya, Oṃ namaḥ Śivāya, Oṃ namaḥ Śivāya, Oṃ namaḥ Śivāya, I focus.

There is only *Oṃ namaḥ Śivāya, Oṃ namaḥ Śivāya, Oṃ namaḥ Śivāya, Oṃ namaḥ Śivāya, Oṃ namaḥ Śivāya, Oṃ namaḥ Śivāya, Oṃ namaḥ Śivāya*, all is well I understand that.

Oṃ namaḥ Śivāya, Oṃ namaḥ Śivāya, Oṃ namaḥ Śivāya, Oṃ namaḥ Śivāya, Oṃ namaḥ Śivāya, Oṃ namaḥ Śivāya, there is a reason for everything, including these volatile emotions.

Oṃ namaḥ Śivāya, Oṃ namaḥ Śivāya, Oṃ namaḥ Śivāya, Oṃ namaḥ Śivāya, Oṃ namaḥ Śivāya, Oṃ namaḥ Śivāya, Oṃ namaḥ Śivāya, Oṃ namaḥ Śivāya, please let me learn from this experience, from these emotions. Let me be open to learning, their purpose in my life. Let me transcend them with your grace.

Oṃ namaḥ Śivāya, Oṃ namaḥ Śivāya, Oṃ namaḥ Śivāya, Oṃ namaḥ Śivāya, Oṃ namaḥ Śivāya, Oṃ namaḥ Śivāya

Oṃ, Oṃ, Oṃ, Oṃ, Oṃ, Oṃ. Oṃ śānti̱ḥ śānti̱ḥ śānti̱ḥ.

To access the live session, click **HERE** or scan the QR code given below:

RELAXATION

This is an invitation to relaxation. One can be seated or lying down for this meditation. The day is done. It is time to come home. The evening sky stretches, hanging like clouds in wagons, waiting to be engulfed by the night.

Thoughts go round in circles in the head like birds trying to find their nest. The cows kick up a dust in their rush to go home, permanently labelling the evening time as *godhūli*, the time of cow dust, twilight. Twilight is a time of reckoning, a time of acceptance. A time that is not noticed, that slips through the cracks between evening and night. That is why it is a time of possibilities: possibilities to gain a new level of understanding about the workings of the mind, to gain new strides in overcoming subtle blocks, resistances.

In this time of possibilities, I learn to relax. Relaxation envelops me like a blanket, like the night enveloping the earth, where it chances to fall. Safe and comfortable, I drop all resistance. I enter into relaxation, which is nothing but my own *swarupa*, my nature.

The feet stretched out, relaxed, comfortable. The bones of the feet carry no tightness and are relaxed. The ball of the foot, the heel: relaxed. The ankle and all the tension that it has held during the day, lets go and softens.

The calf muscles let go. They do not have to hold up the memory of stress, anxiety. They do not have to hold me up anymore. For now, they just flop on the sides, relaxed. No tension, no stress. The knees relax. The thighs, the quadriceps, and the hamstrings follow; nothing is taut. Everything is loose, soft, gentle, and relaxed. Relaxation is me. It is my nature.

The hips relax. The back of the body, beginning from the tailbone, to the lower back, to the mid-back, to the upper back, becomes totally relaxed. No stress, no strain. If there is any discomfort in any of these areas, I let go of all resistance. I let go, I let go. Letting go is letting *Īśvara* be. Letting go is prayer. Letting go is letting God.

The wave of relaxation continues to the front of the body. The pelvic region relaxes and the abdomen follows. All the organs in the abdomen – the intestines, reproductive organs, appendix, kidneys, liver, spleen, pancreas, and gallbladder become relaxed. Relaxation is *Īśvara*, relaxation becomes me.

The stomach relaxes. It gently rises and falls with a breath, but it is at ease. The chest relaxes. The right arm and hand relaxes. The left arm and left hand relaxes. Both shoulders let go of tension completely along with the collar bone in the front. There is no tension. No fear. No worries.

Focus now on the breathing. Breathe gently and easefully. *Prāṇovai Īśvara*. Breathing in, *Īśvara*. *Īśvara* is the incarnation of relaxation. Breathing out, all the stress and tension along with the carbon dioxide. Do this on for a few cycles. Breathe in, *Īśvara,* awareness, relaxation. Breathe out all the stress tension, fears, worries, imperfections, hurts, and guilts. Breathe in, relaxation, *Īśvara*. Breathe out, relaxation, *Īśvara*.

Move your awareness now to the throat area. Let go of all constrictions, fears, and blocks. Relax. Let go, let God. I let *Īśvara* abide in my body. I let *Īśvara* abide in the throat. The face is relaxed, unclenching the jaw. The tongue is resting at the back of the throat, completely relaxed. There is no stress, no tension, and no worry. It is time to let go of the imperfections, time to let go of everything. It is time to relax. Relax the brow, then the cheekbones. Relax the ears, the lips, the teeth, and the whole face. Let go of any tension in the eyelids. When I let go, I let *Īśvara* be. Relaxation is *Īśvara*. Relaxation becomes me.

Focus now on the mind. Let it too become relaxed and easy. Thoughts come, thoughts go. I am in *Īśvara*. *Īśvara* is relaxation. Relaxation becomes me. I don't attach to the thoughts or the worries. It is *svabhāvika*, natural, for them to arise in the mind. As they rise, so they fall, like the tide. Now high, now gone. Born, gone. Thoughts are busy. Born, gone. Gone, born. I am relaxed. Relaxation is *Īśvara*, relaxation becomes me, becomes my *swarupa*.

I connect with the one that is allowing this relaxation, the observer. I observe the body, the mind, the senses. So free. So relaxed. So calm. The observer is free of the stress. The observer is naturally relaxed. The observer is *Īśvara*. Relaxation is *Īśvara*. Relaxation becomes me. *Oṃ śāntiḥ śāntiḥ śāntiḥ*.

To access the live session, click **HERE** or scan the QR code given below:

REMOVING OBSTACLES

The posture is stable, comfortable. I make a space to meditate. The seat is firm. The head, neck and back are in a single straight line. The eyes are softly closed with no wrinkles of tension or force in the eyelids. The hands are gently folded in front of the lap.

Oṃ śuklāmbaradharaṃ viṣṇuṃ śaśivarṇaṃ caturbhujam
prasannavadanaṃ dhyāyet sarvavighnopaśāntaye

The whole day as it unfolds, can be full of obstacles. There are always hidden variables that I cannot account for or anticipate that take me by surprise, sabotaging my endeavors and my efforts. This is the reality.

The law of *karma* keeps unfolding in my life. If I do not face this reality, I become flotsam, a helpless piece of driftwood, in the grip of *pāpa* and *puṇya*, bad and good *karma*, the results thereof.

Intelligent living is taking refuge, asking for help when one needs it. Accepting help can only happen when I acknowledge my helplessness in the face of all the forces that govern my endeavors.

Acknowledging my helplessness is an important aspect of seeking help. Who should I seek help from? From the one who is able to help, from the one who is in charge of karma in my life, in the lives of others, from the one who is capable of removing those obstacles or lessening their blow in my life. *Gaṇāna Īśaḥ*, the Lord of all beings, Gaṇeśa. I pray to this all-pervasive Gaṇeśa, adorned in white garments, whose face is resplendent like the moon, endowed with four arms and a smiling countenance. I meditate upon Lord Gaṇeśa for the resolution of all obstacles in my life today.

Oṃ sumukhāya namaḥ
Oṃ ekadantāya namaḥ

Oṃ kapilāya namaḥ
Oṃ gajakarṇakāya namaḥ
Oṃ lambodarāya namaḥ
Oṃ vikaṭāya namaḥ
Oṃ vighnarājāya namaḥ
Oṃ vināyakāya namaḥ
Oṃ bhālacandrāya namaḥ
Oṃ gajānanāya namaḥ
Oṃ vakratuṇḍāya namaḥ
Oṃ herambāya namaḥ
Oṃ skandapūrvajāya namaḥ
Oṃ varasiddhivināyakasvāmine namaḥ

O Lord Gaṇeśa, May I think of you at the beginning of each day, at the beginning of every endeavor. Make my endeavors, my efforts, bear fruit. Render them free of all obstacles. Give me the strength of mind, of body, and the emotional maturity to learn to face the obstacles that I cannot overcome. *Oṃ śāntiḥ śāntiḥ śāntiḥ.*

To access the live session, click **HERE** or scan the QR code given below:

Hey Bhagavan, melt this inner world of defensiveness and subjectivity. I do not know how to let this go, without basking in your compassionate gaze.

I transcend the chant. I transcend the
silence. I can observe both. I am
consciousness; Īśvara, is
consciousness. The bridge for this as
though alienation is crafted with the
beads of the japamālā.

APPENDIX

TRANSLATION OF ŚLOKAS APPEARING IN THE BOOK

tadviddhi praṇipātena paripraśnena sevayā (BG 4.34)
Learn the truth by prostrating (before the guru), asking relevant questions, and through service.

triguṇākāraṃ trinetraṃ ca triyāyuṣaṃ
trijanma pāpasaṃhāram ekabilvaṃ śivārpaṇaṃ (Bilvāṣṭakam)
A single bilva is offered to Lord Shiva. This leaf embodies the three qualities (of sattva, rajas and tamas). This leaf is like the three eyes (sun, moon and fire). It is like three weapons. It is the destroyer of sins committed in three births.

kṣantavyo me'parādhaḥ Śiva Śiva Śiva bho Śrīmahādeva Śambho (Śivāparādhakṣamāpanastotram)
My omissions and commissions have to be forgiven by you, O Shiva, O Lord of all Lords, who you are the author of everything that is auspicious.

prātaḥ smarāmi hṛdi saṁsphuradātmatattvaṁ
saccitsukhaṁ paramahaṁsagatiṁ turīyam
yatsvapnajāgarasuṣuptimavaiti nityaṁ
tadbrahma niṣkalamahaṁ na ca bhūtasaṅghaḥ
(Prātaḥ-Smaraṇa-Stotram by Adi Shankara)
In the early morning I meditate on the self shining in my heart, which is of the nature of *saccidānanda,* and which is the goal of the most exalted of sages, which knows the three states–dream, waking, and sleeping– that part-less Brahman I am, not this assemblage of the five elements.

Oṃ namaste astu bhagavanviśveśvarāya mahādevāya tryambakāya tripurāntakāya trikāgnikālāya kālāgnirudrāya nīlakaṇṭhāya mṛtyuñjayāya sarveśvarāya sadāśivāya śrīmanmahādevāya namaḥ (Śrī Rudram, Kṛṣṇa Yajurveda, Taittirīya Saṃhitā)
Salutations to you, the Lord of the universe, the Lord of the Lords, the three-eyed one, the bestower of enlightenment, fierce as fire, the Lord of the past, present, and future, the one who ends all, the one who restores order within the world, the one with a blue neck, the defeater of death, the Lord of all beings, the eternal consciousness, to the one who is ever-auspicious.

Oṃ bhūrbhuvaḥ svaḥ tatsaviturvareṇyaṃ bhargo devasya dhīmahi dhiyo yo naḥ pracodayāt (03.62.10 Ṛgveda)
We choose (to invoke) that Effulgent One, which is as brilliant as the sun. May he stimulate our intellects.

na tatra sūryo bhāti na candratārakaṃ, nemā vidyuto bhānti kuto'yamagniḥ, tameva bhāntamanubhāti sarvaṃ tasya bhāsā sarvamidaṃ vibhāti (Kaṭhopaniṣad 2.2.15)
There sun does not shine there, nor do the moon and the stars, nor do (flashes of) lightning shine and much less this fire. When it shines, everything shines after it. The light of all lights (ātman) illuminates everything.

viśvaṃ darpaṇadṛśyamānanagarītulyaṃ nijāntargataṃ
paśyannātmani māyayā bahirivodbhūtaṃ yathā nidrayā
yaḥ sākṣātkurute prabodhasamaye svātmānamevādvayaṃ
tasmai śrīgurumūrtaye nama idaṃ śrīdakṣiṇāmūrtaye
(Dakshinamurti-Stotram by Adi Shankara)
Salutations to Lord Dakshinamurti, the embodiment of the guru, who sees this universe as a dream existing within or as a city in a mirror, but as though appearing externally due to māyāśakti, but upon awakening to the truth of the self sees everything as his own non-dual self.

bījasyāntarivāṅkuro jagadidaṃ prāṅnirvikalpaṃ punaḥ
māyākalpitadeśakālakalanāvaicitryacitrīkṛtam
māyāvīva vijṛmbhayatyapi mahāyogīva yaḥ svecchayā
tasmai śrīgurumūrtaye nama idaṃ śrīdakṣiṇāmūrtaye
(Dakshinamurti-Stotram by Adi Shankara)
Salutations to Lord Dakshinamurti, the embodiment of the guru, who manifests the universe like a great magician or a yogi, which at first is undifferentiated like a sprout within a seed, and which becomes many and varied due to projection of space and time by māyā.

Oṃ hrīṃ dakṣiṇāmūrtaye tubhyaṃ vaṭamūlanivasine
dhyānaikaniratāṅgāya namo rūdraya śambhave hrīṃ Oṃ
(mūla mantra of śrīdakṣiṇāmūrtī Stotram in the Dakshinamurti-Upanishad)
Salutations unto you, O Lord Dakshinamurti, who dwells at the bottom of the banyan tree, who is engrossed in meditation, who is Rudra, the giver of karmaphala, and the bestower of auspiciousness.

śrīrāma rāma rāmeti rame rāme manorame
sahasranāma tattulyaṃ rāma nāma varānane
śrīrāmanāma varānana oṃ nama iti
(72.335, Uttara-khanda of the Padma Purana. It is spoken by Lord Śiva to Parvati)
By chanting the name of Rama, I revel in Rama, which brings joy to the mind. This name is equivalent to chanting a thousand names of Lord Vishnu."

śuklāmbaradharaṃ viṣṇuṃ śaśivarṇaṃ caturbhujam
prasannavadanaṃ dhyāyet sarvavighnopaśāntaye.
I pray to this all -pervasive One, adorned in white garments, whose face is resplendent like the moon, endowed with four arms and a smiling countenance. I meditate upon him for the resolution of all obstacles.

Oṃ sumukhāya namaḥ; salutations to the pleasing one
Oṃ ekadantāya namaḥ; salutation to the single-tusked one
Oṃ kapilāya namaḥ; salutations to Kapila
Oṃ gajakarṇakāya namaḥ; salutations to the elephant-eared one
Oṃ lambodarāya namaḥ; salutations to the big-bellied one
Oṃ vikaṭāya namaḥ; salutations to the large bodied one
Oṃ vighnarājāya namaḥ; salutations to the Lord of obstacles
Oṃ vināyakāya namaḥ; salutations to the Lord in the form of the leader
Oṃ bhālacandrāya namaḥ; saluations to the one with the moon on the head
Oṃ gajānanāya namaḥ; salutations to the elephant-faced one
Oṃ vakratuṇḍāya namaḥ; salutations to the one with the crooked-mouth
Oṃ herambāya namaḥ; salutations to Lord Ganesha
Oṃ skandapūrvajāya namaḥ; salutations to the brother of Skanda
Oṃ varasiddhivināyakasvāmine namaḥ; Salutations to the wish-fulfilling Lord.

GLOSSARY

ābharaṇa	Ornament
abhaya	Fearlessness
abhiṣeka	Ritual bating of deities with sacred liquids
acala	Unmoving
adharma	Improper action
adhibhūta	Centered on the five elements i.e., one's surroundings
adhideva	Centred on God
adhyātma	Centered on the self
Adi Shankara	An ancient teacher and scholar of Vedanta
agni	Fire
aham	I
ahaṅkāra	I-notion, ego
ajñāna	Ignorance
anuloma-viloma	Alternate nostril breathing
aluptadṛk	Constant seer
ānanda	Limitlessness, wholeness
anātman	Not-I, object of cognition
antaḥkaraṇa	Inner-instrument, which includes the mind, intellect, emotions and ego
anugraha	Grace
āratī	Waving of the camphor lamp done at the end of a pūjā
arghya	Water to drink given in a ritual
asaṃhata	Not put together
asaṅga	Uninvolved
asaṅgo'ham	Uninvolved I am
āsana	Seat

astu	May it be so
ātman	The I, the self
ātma-anugraha	Self-grace
ātmajñāna	Self-knowledge
ātmavidyā	Self-knowledge
āvaraṇa	Covering
avatāra	Incarnation of God
aviveka	Non-discrimination
āyatana	Counter of experience
āyudha	Weapon
bhagavān	One endowed with 6 glories or bhaga
bhagavate	Unto Bhagavān
bhagavatī	Goddess
bhakta	A devotee
brahman	That which is limitlessly big, the truth of the self
brahmātmā	Brahman, which is ātman
brahmavidyā	Knowledge of Brahman
Buddha	An avatāra of Bhagavān
buddhaḥ	A wise person
buddhi	Intellect
candana	Sandalwood
carācarātmaka-jagat	The universe filled with moving and stationary things
carācarātmikā nagarī	The city filled with moving and stationary objects
cetṛ	The encourager, in whose presence everything functions
cit	Consciousness
dahanayogya	Fit to be burnt
dama	Restraint
darśana	Vision

deha	Body
deha-vīkṣaṇa	Observing the body
dehin	Indweller of the body
devatā	A God or deity
dharma	A universal matrix of norms
dhārmika	One who follows dharma
dhūpa	Incense
dhyāna	Meditation
dhyātṛ	Meditator
dīpa	Lamp for worship
dravya	Sacred liquids
duḥkha	Sorrow
duḥkhālaya	Abode of sorrow
Durga	Literally, the one who is difficult to reach> Name of a Goddess
dveṣa	Strong prejudices
eko devaḥ	One effulgent consciousness
Ganga	Name of a holy river in India
Ganesha	Lord of all groups, gaṇas
garbhagṛha	The sanctum sanctorum
Gayatri	A meter, the name of a Goddess, a mantra
godhūli	Literally "cow dust," referring to evening time when the cows return home.
Gopala	A name of Lord Krishna
Govinda	The one who is found through words, Lord Krishna
guṇa	Attribute, quality
guru	Remover of self-ignorance, teacher of ātmavidyā
haṃsa	A celestial Swan

hare	Take away
Hari	Name of Lord Vishnu
harināma	Taking the name of the Lord
hṛdayagranthi	Self-Ignorance, literally knot of the heart.
idam	This, referring to something that can be objectified
Īśā	One who is the overlord of all
iṣṭa-devatā	One's favourite form of the Lord
Īśvara	The cause of the universe, the overlord of the creation
iva	As though
jagat	The entire universe starting with one's body-mind-sense complex
jaḍa	Inert
japa	Mental repitition of a mantra
jijñāsā	Desire to know
jīva	A sentient form of Brahman, identified with the physical body
jñāna	Knowledge
jñānin	The knower of Brahman, a wise person
jyotiṣām jyotiḥ	Light of all lights
Kalidasa	An ancient Sanskrit poet
kāma	Desire
karma	Action, also used to refer to consequences of action
karmādhyakṣa	The one who is in charge of the law of karma
karmaphala	Fruit of action
kartṛ	Doer
kartṛtva	Doership
karuṇā	Compassion
kevala	Non-dually one

krodha	Anger
Krishna	Name of the Lord, an avatara
kṣamāpanā	Asking for forgiveness
Kurukshetra	An ancient battlefield
Lalita	Name of a Goddess
lelālayati	Moves, dances
lobha	Greed
mada	Pride
mahāvākya	A sentence that unfolds oneness between jīva and Īśvara
manana	Clarifying the doubts
mānasa-pūjā	Mental worship
mantra	A chant
mātsarya	Jealousy
māyā	The imaginary creative power of Brahman
mithyā	A name given to the empirical reality which depends upon Brahman for its existence
moha	Delusion
mokṣa	Liberation from the sense of bondage
mukta	One who is free
mumukṣutva	The desire for mokṣa
nāḍī-śuddhi	Alternate nostril breathing
naivedya	Ritualistic offering
namaḥ	Salutations, surrender to what is
namaste	Salutations unto you
Nataraja	Lord of dance, an avatara of Lord Śiva
nātha	Lord
Narayana	Name of the Lord, which means "the goal of the human being."

nidhidhyāsana	Contemplation
nirguṇa	Free of all attributes
nirmālya	Dried flower garland
nirvikāra	Changeless
niścala	Unshakable
niṣkala	Part less
nitya	Eternal, not subject to time
niyantṛ	Controller
Oṃ	Sacred sound that refers to Brahman as consciousness and as Īśvara the cause of the universe
paṇcabhūta	Five elements
pāpa	uncomfortable situations faced as a result of violating dharma.
parameśvara	The Lord, Iśvara ,the Creator
paramparā	Lineage
paricchinna	Limited
Parvati	Name of a Goddess
pramātṛ	Knower
prāṇa	Life force
prāṇa-vīkṣaṇa	Observing the breathing
prāṇāyāma	Breathing exercise
prāṇin	A living being
prasāda	Gift from Īśvara
pratibandha	Obstacles
prātibhāsika	Subjective reality
pratyagātmā	Inner-self
pūjā	Ritualistic worship at an altar or temple
puṇya	Comfortable situations as a result of righteous actions

puruṣa	The indweller of the citadel, called the body, jīva and the one that fills up everything, Īśvara
rāga	Strong preferences
rajas	The principle of motion and restlessness, the name of a guṇa
rākṣasa	A person who goes against dharma in pursuit of wealth, power, position.
Rama	Name of the Lord
Ramaṇa Maharsi	A highly renowned Sage
sādhanā	Means of accomplishment, practice
saccidānanda	Limitless existence and awareness resting in a conscious being, definition of ātman
saguṇa	Having attributes or qualities
sākṣīn	Witness
śakti	Power
sama	Equal
śama	Tranquility of the mind
samādhāna	Focus
samagraṃ	Total
samhata	Put together
saṃsāra	A life of becoming
saṃsārin	One who is in the spell of saṃsāra
saṃskṛta	Civilized
sanātana	Everlasting
saṇkalpa	Intention
śāntam	Peaceful
śāntiḥ	Peace
śarīra	Body

sarvabhūtādivāsa	Abides in all beings
sarvabhūtāntarātman	Truth of all creation
sarvabhūteṣu gūḍhāḥ	Abiding, hidden in all beings
sarvātman	The self of all beings
sarvavyāpin	All pervasive.
śāstra	Teachings, sacred texts
sat	Limitless existence
sattva	Godliness, name of a guṇa
satya	Same as sat
śauca	Cleanliness
śikhā	the spire of the temple
śīryamāṇa-svabhāva	Having the nature of disintegration
śiva (as adjective)	Auspicious
śloka	A chant
śnāna	Bath
śraddhā	Trust pending understanding in the paramparā and the guru
śravaṇa	Listening to Vedanta from a teacher
sthāne	In place
sthiram	Steadfast
śuddha	Pure
śuddhi	Purity
sukha	Comfortable
sūkṣma-śarīra,	Subtle body
svabhāvika	Natural
svarūpa	One's own nature
tamasa	Ignorance, sorrow, the name of a guṇa
tasmai	unto that
titikṣā	Forbearance

turīya	Consciousness
tyaja	Give up
uddhara mām	Lift me up
upadeśa	Teaching, instructions
upādhi	That which remaining near an object imparts its attributes to that object. For example: upādhi of a red flower near a crystal makes it appear red.
Upanishad	Revealed texts appearing at the end of the Vedas which unfold the nature of the self as limitlessly whole.
uparati	Letting go
vairāgya	Objectivity, dispassion
vaiśvānara	The Lord in the form of digestive fire
vastu	Reality
Vasudeva	Name of Lord Krishna, lit. the indweller of all
vāyu	Air
Veda	Revealed knowledge
Vedanta	The knowledge of the self occurring at the end of the Vedas.
vibhūti	Glory
viveka	Discrimination
vṛtti	thoughts
Vyasa	Name of an exalted sage, scholar and teacher of Vedanta
yajñopavīta	Sacred thread
yoga	A means for accomplishing something, a way of life
yoga-śāstra	Teachings of karma-yoga

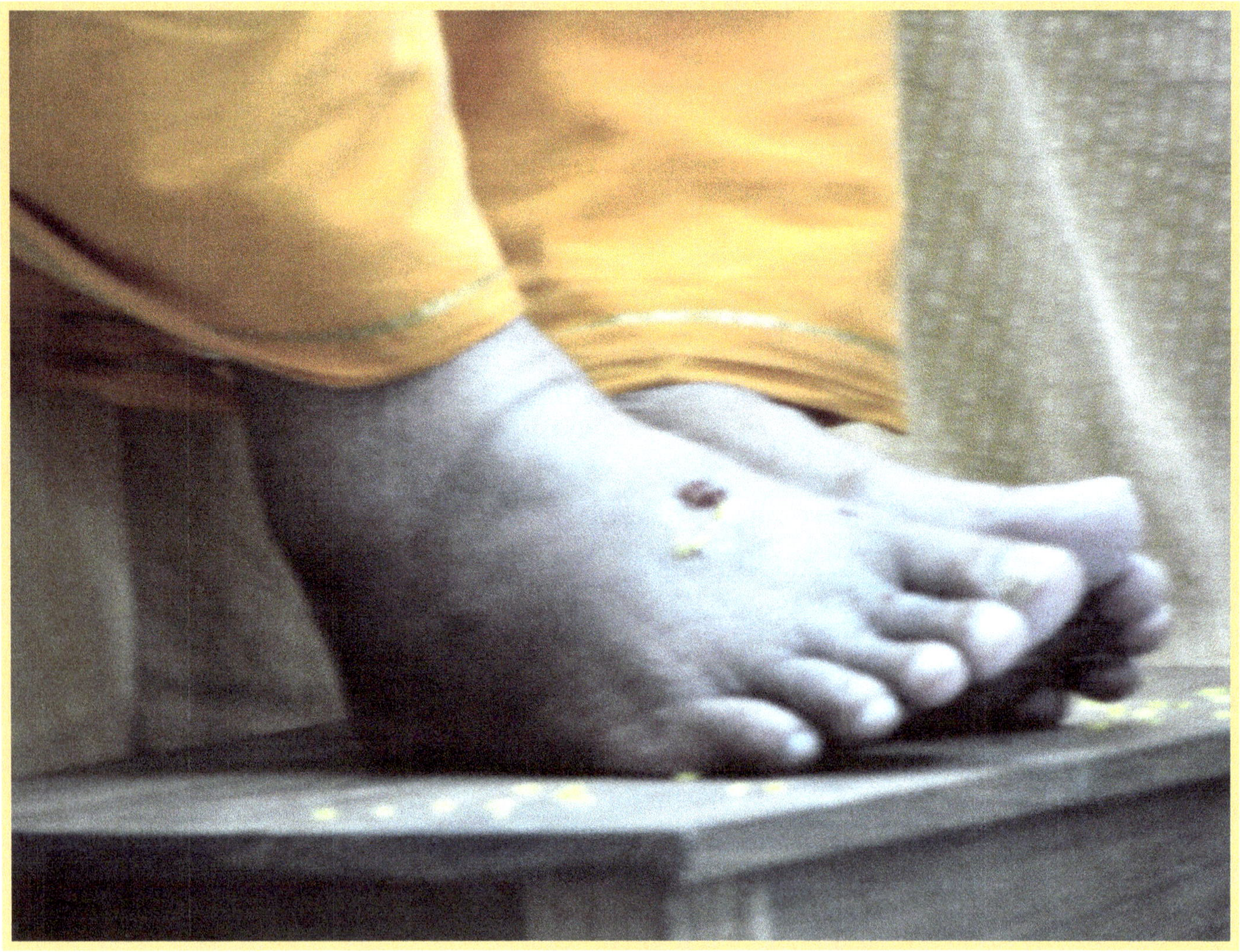

–OM TAT SAT–

oṃ hrīṃ dakṣiṇāmūrtaye tubhyaṃ vaṭamūlanivasine
dhyānaikaniratāṅgāya namo rūdraya śambhave hrīṃ oṃ

–OM TAT SAT–

www.ingramcontent.com/pod-product-compliance
Lightning Source LLC
Chambersburg PA
CBHW080338170426
43194CB00014B/2608
* 9 7 8 1 6 6 6 4 1 4 4 8 6 *